a fantastic voyage into GREEK MYTHOLOGY

Text: **Sofia A. Souli**
Translation: **Chrissi Nerantzi & Adam Frank**
Illustration: **Markos Sigalas**
Cover and 12 Olympic Gods: **Leonard Vassili**
Concept: **Michalis Toubis**

EDITIONS
TOUBI'S
ΕΚΔΟΣΕΙΣ

ATHENS 1998

Greek mythology
is an inexhaustible source of tales and grand myths.
With this illustrated edition, we attempt to present the most important myths
in a way that is entertaining but true to the originals. This publication is also
a unique innovation with regards to comic style, with a combination of illustrations and
photographs which present to the reader a visual jigsaw binding myth
to the reality of ancient Greek art.
Turning the pages will reveal the scenario unfolding, step by step,
in funny scenes via lively pictures. The writer has created the text through inspired
dialogue and the illustrations portray the imagination of the artist.
A reporter is given an assignment by his publisher and is sent on a mission
to Greece. This mission turns out to be the ticket for a dive into antiquity where
he experiences a dreamlike journey through the myths. So just follow him
and have the adventure of a lifetime.

The publisher

All words in bold are explained in the glossary (page 56)

Copyright © 1998 MICHALIS TOUBIS EDITIONS S.A. 519 Vouliagmenis Ave., Ilioupolis, 16341
Tel: (01) 9923876 - FAX: (01) 9923867 INTERNET: http://www.toubis.gr

ISBN 960-540-253-X

'THE SEARCHER' MAGAZINE

EDITOR

KNOCK! KNOCK!

AH! CHERCHER. I CALLED YOU IN BECAUSE THEY SAY YOU'RE GOOD AT YOUR JOB. I WANT A JUICY STORY ON GREEK MYTHOLOGY FOR OUR NEXT ISSUE. SO WHY DON'T YOU HOP OVER TO GREECE AND CHECK THINGS OUT ON THE SPOT. BUT WE NEED THE STORY QUICK.

SURE, I'LL GO, BUT WHAT'S THE RUSH? ARE YOU WORRIED THAT MAYBE WE'LL MISS...THE MOMENT? THAT STORY'LL BE JUST AS FRESH A MONTH FROM NOW.

HMPF! I FORGOT TO TELL YOU, THE PLANE LEAVES IN THREE HOURS.

OK! BOSS.

VOOOM

ATHENS, A FEW HOURS LATER.

GOSH, I'M TIRED.

WHA...?! WHAT HAPPENED??! WHERE AM I??!

IN THE BEGINNING, THERE WAS NOTHING. EVERYTHING WAS CHAOS, AND OUT OF THIS CHAOS, NIGHT WAS BORN.

REALLY?!

YES! AND FROM NIGHT CAME DAY.

HMM...CLEAR AS MUD!

THAT'S ALL THERE WAS UNTIL URANUS MADE A PLAY FOR GAIA. THEY HIT IT OFF AND THE MYTHICAL TITANS SHOWED THEIR FACES, THOSE LITTLE BRATS. THEN...

QUITE A ROGUE THAT URANUS!

...OTHERS WERE BORN: OCEANUS, HYPERION, COEUS, IAPETUS, CRONUS, RHEA, THE HECATONCHIERES, THE CYCLOPES...

ENOUGH! ENOUGH! OK! OK! HOW COULD I POSSIBLY REMEMBER ANY MORE?

BUT GAIA...ALSO FIXED HERSELF UP WITH PONTUS, WHO WRAPPED HIMSELF AROUND HER AND AFTER HE GAVE HER A LITTLE...REFRESHMENT, THERE WERE MORE LITTLE BRATS ON THE WAY.

JUST A REFRESHMENT? SHE WAS INSATIABLE!

CRONUS RULED AFTER HE MADE HIS FATHER, URANUS, REDUNDANT...

DON'T TELL ME HE CUT OFF...WHAT I THINK HE CUT OFF??

EXACTLY!

HE MARRIED RHEA WHO WAS VERY PROLIFIC, BUT...CRONUS WAS AFRAID OF LOSING HIS THRONE TO HIS CHILDREN, SO HE ATE THEM.

RHEAAA! BRING ME A SNACK. WHERE'S THAT KID THAT WAS BORN TODAY?

THAT MONSTER'S EATEN ALL MY CHILDREN. THIS ROCK WILL SAVE MY LITTLE ZEUS.

ZEUS GREW UP QUICKLY, HIDDEN IN A CAVE ON CRETE WHERE HE WAS CARED FOR BY THE CURETES WHO BANGED ON THEIR SHIELDS TO DROWN OUT HIS CRIES SO CRONUS WOULDN'T HEAR HIM..

A FEW YEARS LATER, HE CAME BACK TO HIS FATHER.

SPIT OUT MY BOTHERS AND SISTERS QUICK, OR YOU'LL BE SORRY!

THEN ZEUS, ASSISTED BY HIS BROTHERS AND SISTERS, AS WELL AS THE HECATONCHIERES AND THE CYCLOPES, DEFEATED HIS FATHER CRONUS AND THE TITANS IN THE GREAT TITANOMACHY, AND BECAME CHAMPION.

OI! WHO'S PULLING MY HEAD?

LET'S GET ORGANIZED CHAPS. I HAVEN'T THROWN A STONE YET.

OLYMPUS

OTHRYS

EVER SINCE THEN, ATLAS HAS BEEN PUNISHED FOR BEING IN THE ENEMY CAMP, AND MUST BEAR THE WEIGHT OF THE EARTH...IT MAKES ME DIZZY JUST TO THINK ABOUT IT.

AFTER SOME TIME, THE GIGANTOMACHY FOLLOWED AND ZEUS WON AGAIN. ASSISTED BY HIS DAUGHTER ATHENA AND THE DEMIGOD HERACLES.

IF IT WASN'T FOR HERA-CLES...WEREN'T THERE ANY PEOPLE BACK THEN? ONLY GODS?

HMMM...YES THERE WERE, BUT THEY WERE STILL WEAK.

EPIMETHEUS WAS THE SON OF THE TITAN IAPETUS WHO HAD GIVEN HIM ALL THE VIRTUES TO SHARE OUT...BUT EPIMETHEUS WAS UNFAIR AND GAVE MANKIND'S STRENGTH TO THE ANIMALS.

BUT HIS BROTHER PROMETHEUS TOOK WISDOM FROM ATHENA AND GAVE IT TO MANKIND, AND THEN STOLE FIRE FROM THE GODS AND GAVE IT TO THEM AS A GIFT.

REMEMBER, WHEN YOU BUILD A BARBE-CUE IN THE WOODS, ALWAYS PUT SOME STONES AROUND THE FIRE SO YOU DON'T BURN THE PLACE DOWN!

BUT ZEUS PUNISHED PROMETHEUS, CHAINING HIM TO THE TOP OF A MOUNTAIN IN THE CAUCASUS WITH AN EAGLE TEARING HIS LIVER OUT EVERY NIGHT...

I THINK I'LL HAVE LIVER AGAIN TODAY!

...UNTIL HERACLES FREED HIM SOME YEARS LATER.

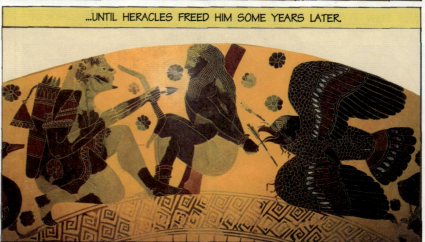

THE MOST IMPORTANT GODS OF THE ANCIENT GREEKS WERE THOSE KNOWN AS THE TWELVE GODS OF OLYMPUS. THEY HAD GREAT POWER BUT ALL THE HUMAN WEAKNESSES AS WELL. THEY DRANK NECTAR, A DIVINE BEVERAGE, AND ATE AMBROSIA.

DID THEY EAT SOUVLAKIA WITH TZATZIKI TOO?? HEE! HEE! HEE!

MANKIND MADE SACRIFICES TO THEM AND COMMUNICATED WITH THEM THROUGH PRIESTS, SEERS AND ORACLES.

YOU CAN'T GET AWAY FROM THEM!

I AM THE SEER CALCHAS; I SEE ALL AND I OGLE ALL...TODAY THE KING'S SNAKE SLUNK OFF IN A STRANGE DIRECTION. A BAD OMEN. BAAAAD!

DON'T WORRY FRIENDS, IF YOU WANT TO KNOW YOUR FUTURE, I'LL GLADLY WATCH THE MOVEMENT OF YOUR SNAKE.

YOU THINK HE'S ONE OF THEM PEEPING TOMS?

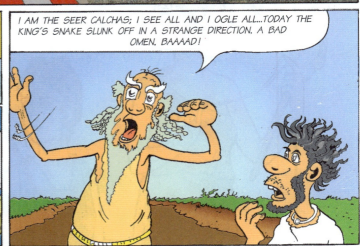

PYTHIA, A PRIESTESS AT DELPHI, WAS GIVING ADVICE WHILST ENTRANCED.

MY DEAR PYTHIA, CAN YOU READ THE COFFEE GROUNDS IN THIS CUP TOO?

HEY, LIKE I CAN READ THE CUP, A GLASS OR THE POT, I'M SO STONED UP HERE ON MY DELPHIC TRIPOD, I MIGHT EVEN SING SOME CAROLS, MAN.

WHAT DOES CHRYSIPPUS, THE ORACLE OF APOLLO, SAY?

HE SAYS...HE SAYS...WE SHOULDN'T START A WAR. IT'S NOT A GOOD MONTH FOR IT.

LOOK! THERE'S THE BLIND SEER, THE RESPECTED TIRESIAS, WHO SEES EVERYTHING.

HE CAN'T EVEN SEE HIS NOSE IN FRONT OF HIS FACE.

7

BUT, I STILL HAVEN'T TOLD YOU ABOUT THE OLYMPIAN GODS ONE BY ONE.

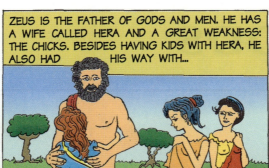

ZEUS IS THE FATHER OF GODS AND MEN. HE HAS A WIFE CALLED HERA AND A GREAT WEAKNESS: THE CHICKS. BESIDES HAVING KIDS WITH HERA, HE ALSO HAD HIS WAY WITH...

MAIA, WHO GAVE BIRTH TO HERMES. THEN HE CAME ON TO SEMELE AND DIONYSUS WAS BORN, WHO WAS A LITTLE PREMATURE BECAUSE HIS MOTHER WAS SHOCKED TO DEATH ONE NIGHT WHEN ZEUS...

BARGED INTO THE BEDROOM, DISPLAYING HIS MAJESTY WITH ALL HIS HORSES, AND AT THE BIG MOMENT, STRUCK HER WITH A THUNDERBOLT FROM ABOVE. LATER ON, DURING ANOTHER AFAIR, HE FELL IN LOVE WITH LETO WHO GAVE BIRTH TO APOLLO AND ARTEMIS.

YEAAAH!

YEAH, BUT WHAT ABOUT HERA'S JEALOUSY?

WHAT A BEAUTIFUL SWAN! LET'S RUN AND CATCH IT.

DON'T!! IT'S ZEUS IN DISGUISE. HE'S AFTER LEDA.

HAVE YOU HEARD? THEY SAY THAT ZEUS TOOK THAT YOUNG **GANYMEDE** UP TO OLYMPUS TO BE HIS...CUP BEARER.

WATCH WHAT YOU SAY. HE WOULDN'T THINK TWICE ABOUT STRIKING YOU IN THE HEAD WITH A THUNDERBOLT.

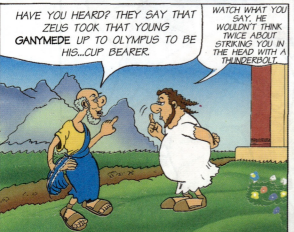

OH! OH!...HERE COMES MADAM HERA.

I HOPE SHE DIDN'T HEAR WHAT WE SAID.

A BULL JUST CAME RACING OVER THE SEA WITH EUROPA ON HIS BACK AND HIS FACE LOOKED AN AWFUL LOT LIKE ZEUS TO ME.

NOOO!! YOU'RE IMAGINING THINGS. YOURE IMAGINING THINGS!

ZEUS LOVED THE BEAUTIFUL EUROPA. IN ORDER TO GET NEAR HER HE TRANSFORMED HIMSELF INTO A BEAUTIFUL WHITE BULL AND LAID DOWN IN FRONT OF HER. EUROPA BEGAN TO PLAY WITH THE BULL AND AT ONE POINT SHE SAT ON ITS BACK WHEREUPON THE BULL SPED AWAY OVER THE SEA WITH HER DESPITE HER SCREAMS. THE BULL TRAVELLED A LONG WAY AND FINALLY REACHED THE SPRING OF GORTYNIA WHERE THE PAIR COUPLED.

WHO'S THAT WOMAN OVER THERE WITH THE SPEAR AND THE HELMET?

THAT'S ZEUS' DAUGHTER ATHENA, THE GOD-DESS OF WISDOM. SHE JUST GOT BACK FROM HER CONTEST WITH POSEIDON. SHE'S PLEASED BECAUSE SHE WON AND THE CITY OF ATTICA WILL NOW BEAR HER NAME.

LONG LIVE ATHENA!

THIS IS OUR MAN ON THE SPOT, REPORTING BACK TO THE STUDIO...LADIES AND GENTLE-MEN, AT THIS MOMENT, THE PANATHENAIC PROCESSION HAS JUST BEGUN.

SOUVLAKIA

THE PARTHENON, THE TEMPLE ON THE ACROPOLIS, IS DEDICATED TO THE GODDESS ATHENA. EVERY YEAR, AS TODAY, THE PANATHENAEA IS HELD IN HER HONOUR.

THE CELEBRATIONS CONTINUE WITH RACES AND ATH-LETIC EVENTS...THE CROWDS CHEER ON THE ATH-LETES.

LADIES AND GENTLEMEN, THE PANA-THENAEA IS A ROARING SUCCESS AND PUBLIC SUPPORT HAS BEEN OVERWHELMING. IN JUST ONE DAY 10,000 SOUVLAKIA, 7,000 AMPHORAS OF WINE FROM MESO-GEION AND 500 OKAS OF PISTA-CHIOS HAVE BEEN CONSUMED. NOT TO MENTION THE ROASTED PUMPKIN SEEDS.

BLAM!

I'VE NEVER UNDER-STOOD THE SCIENCE FICTION OF THE TV!!!

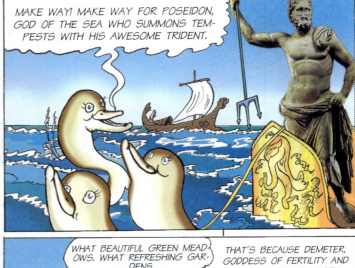

MAKE WAY! MAKE WAY FOR POSEIDON, GOD OF THE SEA WHO SUMMONS TEM-PESTS WITH HIS AWESOME TRIDENT.

WHAT BEAUTIFUL GREEN MEAD-OWS. WHAT REFRESHING GAR-DENS.

THAT'S BECAUSE DEMETER, GODDESS OF FERTILITY AND AGRICULTURE, IS HAPPY AGAIN. HER DAUGHTER PERSEPHONE IS BACK...

...FROM THE UNDERWORLD WHERE PLUTO, GOD OF HADES, HAD IMPRISONED HER. HE GRABBED HER ONE DAY SECRETLY FROM HER MOTHER AND HID HER AWAY.

ELEUSIS

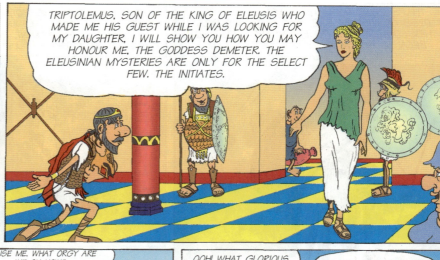

TRIPTOLEMUS, SON OF THE KING OF ELEUSIS WHO MADE ME HIS GUEST WHILE I WAS LOOKING FOR MY DAUGHTER, I WILL SHOW YOU HOW YOU MAY HONOUR ME, THE GODDESS DEMETER. THE ELEUSINIAN MYSTERIES ARE ONLY FOR THE SELECT FEW. THE INITIATES.

GREAT ZEUS!

DID THE PRIESTESS STRIP?

BY THE CLUB OF HERACLES, I'LL SHOW YOU!

EXCUSE ME. WHAT ORGY ARE WE ON NOW?

WILL THE MATINEE CROWD PLEASE MAKE WAY FOR THE EVENING CROWD.

TAP TAP

OOH! WHAT GLORIOUS MUSIC IS THIS WHICH STROKES MY LITTLE EAR?

IT'S THE GOD APOLLO PLAYING HIS LYRE.

A FANTASTIC GOD! NOT ONLY OF MUSIC BUT OF LIGHT TOO. HE AND HIS SISTER ARTEMIS WERE. BORN ON DELOS AND THEIR PARENTS WERE LETO AND ZEUS.

THAT ZEUS IS REALLY SOMETHING!

APOLLO'S ALWAYS FALLING IN LOVE WITH THE BEAUTIFUL YOUNG GIRLS. AND THE YOUNG BOYS TOO.

AHA! TELL ME MORE.

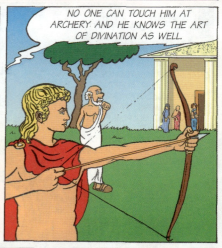

NO ONE CAN TOUCH HIM AT ARCHERY AND HE KNOWS THE ART OF DIVINATION AS WELL.

LOOK, THERE'S HIS SLENDER LITTLE SISTER ARTEMIS, GODDESS OF THE HUNT...WHAT A BABE!

SHHH! IF SHE HEARS YOU, YOU'VE HAD IT. DO YOU KNOW WHAT HAPPENED TO **ACTEON** WHEN HE SAW HER BATHING?

SHE TURNED HIM INTO A DEER AND SET HIS OWN DOGS ON HIM.

JUST FOR A LITTLE PEEK?

WHAT'S THAT ABOVE US? IT DOESN'T LOOK LIKE A BIRD.

OR A HANG-GLIDER EITHER.

KEEP QUIET! IT'S THE GOD HERMES, A REAL SCOUNDREL. WHO KNOWS WHAT THAT CROOK'S UP TO TODAY?

HE'S THE SON OF ZEUS AND MAIA, THE GODS' MESSENGER AND A MERCHANT...BUT WHAT A MERCHANT! A REAL SLIGHT-OF-HAND ARTIST!

THAT'S THREE FOR THE OIL AND THREE FOR THE VINEGAR...AND SIX FOR THE OIL AND VINEGAR, THAT'S TWELVE ALTOGETHER.

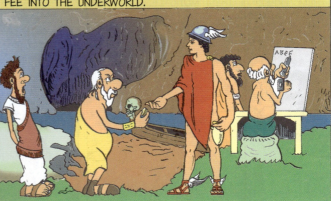

HE ALSO ACCOMPANIES THE DEAD TO HADES AND POCKETS HALF THE MONEY THEY TAKE WITH THEM FOR THEIR ENTRANCE FEE INTO THE UNDERWORLD.

OH NO! IT'S MADAM APHRODITE...COVER YOUR EYES AND EARS. THAT WOMAN COULD TEMPT EVEN A SAINT. SHE'S THE GODDESS OF LOVE YOU KNOW...

WHO ARE THEY WITH HER?

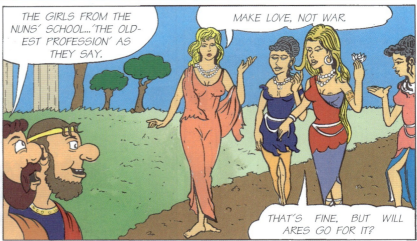

THE GIRLS FROM THE NUNS' SCHOOL...'THE OLD-EST PROFESSION' AS THEY SAY.

MAKE LOVE, NOT WAR.

THAT'S FINE, BUT WILL ARES GO FOR IT?

I FIGHT WITH MY SANDAL, THAT'S JUST ME, BUT I LIKE TO FLIRT WITH HUNKS LIKE ADONIS.

WHAT A HUNK! WHO IS HE? MR WORLD?

SIGH! THE BEST ONES ALWAYS LOSE THEIR WAY.

BEING THE BLACKSMITH AND MASTER CRAFTSMAN HE IS, HEPHAESTUS MADE AN INVISIBLE NET. HE TOLD HER HE WAS GOING OUT AND SHE TOLD HER BOYFRIEND TO COME RIGHT OVER.

HERE COMES ARES, GOD OF WAR HE CAN BARELY LIFT HIS FEET LET ALONE HIS SHIELD. TOO MUCH OVERTIME...

...NOT TO MENTION THE DIRTY TRICK HEPHAESTUS PLAYED ON HIM.

WHAT TRICK?

AAA! YOU DON'T KNOW? WELL, HEPHAESTUS IS THE HUSBAND OF APHRODITE. SOMEONE TIPPED HIM OFF THAT SHE WAS HAVING A THING WITH ARES.

HEPHAESTUS CAME BACK SUDDENLY, FOUND THEM IN BED, AND THREW THE NET OVER THEM, FREEZING THEM MOTIONLESS AT THE CRITICAL MOMENT...

...THEN HE CALLED ON THE GODS AND ZEUS. HE'D MADE THE LOVERS LOOK LIKE FOOLS. HE COMPLAINED.

LOOK AT THE SORT OF WIFE YOU'VE GIVEN ME.

HE'S A SLY FELLOW THAT HEPHAESTUS, EVEN IF HE HAS GOT A LIMP. HE REVEALED THE SECRET AND GOT ONE OVER ON ARES WHO IS ALL BRAWN AND NO BRAIN. HOW WOULD YOU FEEL, HERMES, IF SOMEONE HUMILIATED YOU LIKE THAT?

OH MAN ! JUST LET ME GET INTO BED WITH APHRODITE AND ALL THE GODS, GODDESSES AND THE WHOLE WORLD CAN WATCH FOR ALL I CARE.

HA! HA!

HOWEVER, HEPHAESTUS IS THE DIVINE CRAFTSMAN AND FROM HIS WORKSHOP COME THE MOST WONDERFUL THINGS: STATUES, SUITS OF ARMOUR FOR GODS AND HEROES, THRONES AND HE EVEN MADE THE MOST PERFECT FEMALE STATUE, **PANDORA**, TO WHOM, FOR HER MANY VIRTUES, ZEUS GAVE THE BREATH OF LIFE.

...AND SHE MARRIED EPIMETHEUS...WHO WASN'T QUITE ALL THERE...

BLAH! BLAH! BLAH!

AS FOR ARES. WHAT CAN I SAY? HE WAS INVOLVED IN ALL THE ATHLETIC SPORTS. WHEREVER THERE WAS A WAR, HE WAS IN IT AND WHERE THERE WAS A HORSE, HE WAS ON IT.

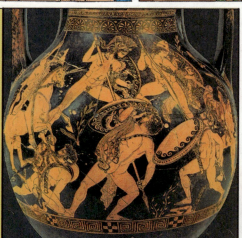

HESTIA WAS A GOOD HOUSEKEEPER BUT STILL AN OLD MAID.

LIKE A GOOD BROTHER, ZEUS TOLD HER "PUT ON SOME MAKE UP, DRESS NICE, PUT A WIGGLE IN YOUR WALK, GET OUT OF THE HOUSE AND FIND YOURSELF A MAN".

BUT SHE WOULDN'T LISTEN. SHE SAYS SHE'S GOING TO DEVOTE HER LIFE TO THE FAMILY.

GOOD FOR HER! ME TOO. WITH ALL MY WISDOM I PREFER THE BACHELOR LIFE.

APART FROM THE TWELVE GODS OF OLYMPUS, HOWEVER, THERE WERE ALSO SOME OTHER, LESSER GODS WHO WERE PRETTY COOL.

LIKE WHO?

LIKE DIONYSUS THE SON OF ZEUS BY SEMELE FOR WHOM HE PUT ON THE SHOW WE MENTIONED EARLIER

THAT GOD OF WINE AND MERRIMENT WAS SOME DRINKER!

OPAA! ALL THE BARRELS TO THE DANCE FLOOR!!

QUICK SILENUS, OPEN ANOTHER BARREL.

ASCLEPIUS WAS THE GOD OF MEDICINE. HE TREATED ALL ILLNESSES.

HEY, WHO'S THAT?

THE SNAKE-MAN, MY STAR SIGN.

WHAT DO YOU MEAN YOUR STAR SIGN? WASN'T HE ON THE 10,000 DRACHMA NOTE.

CUT IT OUT. HELIOS IS COMING.

TSK! THAT OLD GOSSIP!

WOAH! BE CAREFUL OR YOU'LL FALL IN THAT HOLE. ALL PLUTON, GOD OF THE UNDERWORLD NEEDS IS ONE CHANCE. DOWN THERE, IN HIS DREADFUL KINGDOM, EVERYTHING IS...

HE RUNS AROUND ALL DAY LIGHTING UP THE EARTH AND BRINGING EVERYTHING OUT INTO THE OPEN.

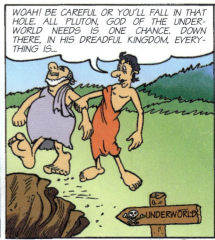

UNDERWORLD

...DARK AND COBWEBBY.

OF COURSE!

YOU MEAN THE DEAD END UP THERE WHETHER THEY'RE GOOD OR BAD?

GOSH! THEN I DON'T SEE MUCH OF A FUTURE FOR OUR RELIGION.

WHAT BEAUTIFUL MUSIC...WHO'S PLAYING THE PAN PIPES SO WELL?

THE GOD PAN, WHO IS HALF GOAT.

...AND WHO PROTECTS THE SHEPHERDS AND THEIR FLOCKS WHILST HE HAS HIS WAY WITH THE NYMPHS AND SHEPHERDESSES.

TEE! HEE! DON'T THE GOATS GET JEALOUS?

WATCH OUT! DON'T LET ANY OF THOSE ARROWS COME NEAR YOU.

WHAT'S GOING ON?

IT'S THAT WINGED MISCHIEF-MAKER, EROS, APHRODITE'S SON. IF ONE OF HIS ARROWS FINDS YOU IN THE HEART YOU'VE HAD IT!

WE DON'T NEED ANY HEARTACHE AROUND HERE.

15

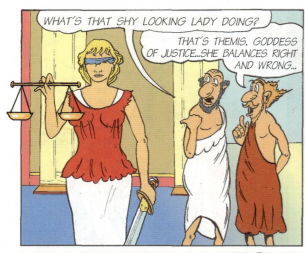

WHAT'S THAT SHY LOOKING LADY DOING?

THAT'S THEMIS, GODDESS OF JUSTICE...SHE BALANCES RIGHT AND WRONG...

...BLINDFOLDED.

UHH, I THINK SHE'S PEEKING. ARE YOU SURE THAT BLINDFOLD IS TIGHT ENOUGH?

WHAT IF SOMEONE SLIPS PAST HER?

NO ONE ESCAPES DIVINE JUSTICE.

AND EVEN IF THEY DID GET PAST THEMIS, THE ERINYES WOULD HUNT HIM DOWN AND HE'D NEVER HAVE A MOMENT'S PEACE.

WOW! WHAT A LOT OF GODS! HOW DO YOU GET ALONG WITH ALL OF THEM? IS IT POSSIBLE TO WHEN THEY FIGHT AMONGST THEMSELVES?

I TELL YOU, BETWEEN YOU AND ME, I SACRIFICE TO THEM ALL JUST TO BE ON THE SAFE SIDE.

SO THERE WERE ALL-POWERFUL GODS WHO DETERMINED THE FATES OF US WEAK HUMANS.

AHH, YOU DON'T UNDERSTAND. THERE WERE HEROES TOO...

...SONS OF GODS AND MORTALS, DEMIGODS AS THEY WERE CALLED, WHO MADE THINGS EASIER.

FIRST AND GREATEST WAS HERACLES, THE SON OF ZEUS AND ALCMENE, WHO WAS BORN IN THEBES.

WAAAA!

WHEN HE WAS STILL A BABY, THAT JEALOUS GODDESS HERA SENT TWO SNAKES TO KILL HIM IN HIS CRADLE. BUT HERACLES...

...STRANGLED THEM WITH HIS BARE HANDS.

TOUGH LITTLE NIPPER, EH?

WHEN HE GREW UP, TWO WOMEN CAME ON TO HIM.

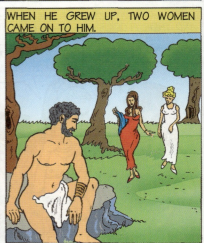

ONE OF THEM, THE BAD ONE, WAS ALL DECKED OUT AND PAINTED AND SHE SPUN HIM A STORY ABOUT HOW HE SHOULD FOLLOW HER FOR A WONDERFUL, EASY LIFE.

PARTIES, CHEAP BOUZOUKI JOINTS, SMOKING, LYING AROUND, AND ALL THE REST.

THE OTHER ONE WAS SWEET, ATTRACTIVE, WORE A WHITE DRESS AND SHE GAVE IT TO HIM STRAIGHT, VERY CLEARLY.

THERE'LL BE NO LYING AROUND, NO PARTIES, JUST HARD WORK AND, IN TIME, YOU'LL WIN...

...THE RESPECT OF MANKIND. IF YOU FOLLOW ME, EVERYONE WILL COME TO KNOW THE NAME OF HERACLES.

WHAT'S YOUR NAME?

I'M COMING WITH YOU!

ARETI*

*VIRTUE

BUT HERA, IN HER JEALOUSY, LATER SENT HIM INTO A MAD RAGE IN WHICH HE KILLED HIS CHILDREN BY HIS FIRST WIFE.

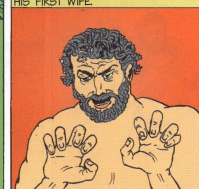

AS A PUNISHMENT, AN ORACLE SENT HIM TO HIS COUSIN EURYSTHEUS TO BE HIS SERVANT.

KING EURYSTHEUS WAS A REAL NUT-CASE AND HE TOOK IT OUT ON HERACLES.

GO AND KILL THE NEMEAN LION.

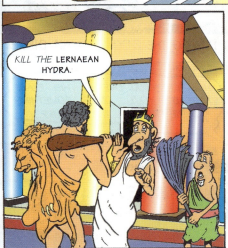

KILL THE LERNAEAN HYDRA.

THE LERNAEAN HYDRA HAD RAISED ITS HEAD...HEADS, ABOUT A HUNDRED OF THEM...IN ANGER AND WAS DESTROYING CROPS AND SPREADING DISEASE.

17

WITH IOLAUS' HELP, HERACLES DEFEATED IT.

IOLAUS, THE TORCH QUICK!

BRING ME THE CYRENEAN HIND.

GO...GO AND...UH...GO AND CATCH THE ERYMANTHIAN BOAR.

EURYSTHEUS, YOUR PREZZIE.

BUT, OVERCOME WITH FEAR, EURYSTHEUS HID IN A PITHOS.

LATER, HERACLES WENT HUNTING THE STYMPHALIAN BIRDS.

UNITED CHICKENS ARE NEVER PLUCKED*

GOODBYE MY BEAUTIES.

*TACTICAL MANOEUVRE: LOSE THE BATTLE, NOT YOUR MORALE.

IN THE KINGDOM OF ELIS ON ANOTHER MISSION.

HOW CAN YOU LIVE IN THIS PLACE AUGEAS? YOU'LL CATCH SOMETHING AND DIE FROM ALL THAT MANURE...

PONG PONG

...AND YOUR FIELDS NEED THE FERTILIZER.

THERE'S NOTHING I CAN DO. DON'T TELL ME YOU CAN DO SOMETHING? IF YOU CAN, I'LL GIVE YOU HALF MY KINGDOM.

BY CHANGING THE COURSE OF THE ALPHEIOS AND PINEIOS RIVERS, THE FLOW OF THE RIVERS WILL CLEAN...

...THE PLACE AND SPREAD MANURE OVER THE PLAIN OF ELIS TO MAKE IT MORE FERTILE.

MY REWARD!!

FORGET IT. I ONLY AGREED BECAUSE I DIDN'T EXPECT YOU TO DO IT.

HERACLES GOT HIS REVENGE ON AUGEAS. HE FOUGHT HIM AND WON AND MADE HIS SON KING.

OH! OH! HERE COMES TROUBLE.

GO OUT AND CATCH THE MAN-EATING HORSES OF DIOMEDES.

AND THEN WHAT YOU NUT-CASE? YOU'VE NEVER EVEN RIDDEN A WOODEN HORSE ON A MERRY-GO-ROUND.

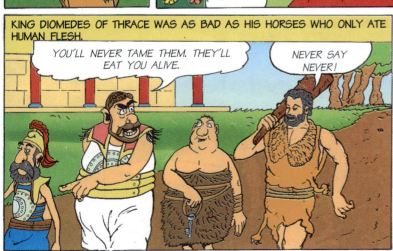

KING DIOMEDES OF THRACE WAS AS BAD AS HIS HORSES WHO ONLY ATE HUMAN FLESH.

YOU'LL NEVER TAME THEM. THEY'LL EAT YOU ALIVE.

NEVER SAY NEVER!

THE BOSS WAS DELICIOUS AND IT DIDN'T SEEM LIKE HE WOULD BE.

PHEW! I'M SICK OF EATING MEAT. FROM NOW ON I'M GOING TO BE A VEGETARIAN.

...AND THE HERO RETURNED LEADING THE HORSES HE HAD TAMED.

AND WHAT A HERO !! HE EVEN DEFEATED THANATOS* AT **PHERES** TO KEEP HIM FROM TAKING ALCESTES, THE WIFE OF HIS FRIEND ADMITOS, TO THE KINGDOM OF THE UNDERWORLD.

HEY! HEY! EASY ON THE BONES FRIEND!

GREAT ZEUS. WHAT KIND OF MORTAL IS THIS? OR DID YOU HAVE A...HAND IN IT TOO?

*DEATH

AT ANOTHER COMMAND FROM EURYSTHEUS, HE BROUGHT THE **CRETAN BULL** TO ARGOLIS.

SHUT UP AND SWIM.

MOOOO!

DADDY, THE **AMAZON** HIPPOLYTE IS WEARING A TOTALLY WICKED **BELT** THAT ARES GAVE HER AND I WANT IT.

HERACLES! DID YOU HEAR WHAT MY DAUGHTER SAID? SHE WANTS THAT BELT WITH ITS SQUILLION CARATS. AS LONG AS IT EXISTS, SHE HAS TO HAVE IT.

WHY SO MUCH FIGHTING AND SO MUCH BLOOD, HIPPOLYTE? GIVE ME THE BELT NOW SO I CAN DO MY JOB AND I'LL GET YOU AN EVEN BETTER ONE FROM CHRISTIAN DIOR.

IT'S A DEAL, BIG BOY!

THAT **GERYON** OUT WEST MAY BE THE BIGGEST FREAK AROUND WITH HIS THREE BODIES, SIX ARMS, THREE HEADS AND HIS WINGS, BUT HE ALSO HAS SOME WELL-FED OXEN!

WATCH YOUR BLOOD PRESSURE, BOSS.

I WANT THEM!

DONE.

HE MISSES HIS FAMILY.

SPROING! SPROING

A SHORT WHILE LATER.

KING, PREPARE A SACRIFICE TO HERA. YOU'VE GOT YOUR WISH. EVERY SINGLE ONE. HA! HA! HA!

ARE ALL THE COWS HERE?

MOOOO

I WANT THE GOLDEN APPLES OF THE HESPERIDES.

CAN'T YOU EAT SOME OTHER FRUIT TODAY?

NO! I WANT THOSE.

THE GOLDEN APPLES WERE IN THE GARDEN OF THE HESPERIDES WHERE THEY WERE GUARDED BY THE THREE NYMPHS.

THERE HE MET ATLAS, WHO WAS HOLDING UP THE SKY.

I'M IMPRESSED, ATLAS! YOU MUST BE QUITE A MAN TO HOLD THE SKY ON YOUR BACK. LOOK, I'LL GIVE YOU A REST FOR A WHILE, GO AND PICK ME A COUPLE OF THOSE GOLDEN DELICIOUSES FROM THE GARDEN.

LOOK FRIEND, I KIND OF LIKE BEING FREE, SO I'LL TELL YOU WHAT, I'LL GO AND TAKE YOUR APPLES FOR YOU.

OK, BUT I'M NOT QUITE COMFORTABLE YET. TAKE OVER FOR A COUPLE OF MINUTES WHILE I GO GET A CUSHION...

RATS! HE TRICKED ME...

UNBELIEVABLE! NO MATTER WHERE I SEND HIM, HE COMES BACK ALIVE, THE WILDEST MONSTERS, THE WORST BAD GUYS AND ON SUCH DANGEROUS TRIPS.

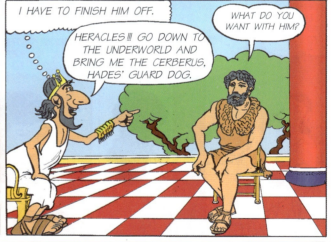

I HAVE TO FINISH HIM OFF.

HERACLES!!! GO DOWN TO THE UNDERWORLD AND BRING ME THE CERBERUS, HADES' GUARD DOG.

WHAT DO YOU WANT WITH HIM?

TO TAKE HIM TO THE PARK...I DON'T KNOW...I DON'T WANT HIM FOR ANYTHING...JUST BRING HIM...OK?

HERACLES FOUGHT WITH THE THREE-HEADED GUARD DOG OF THANATOS WHICH HAD THREE HEADS, MANY SNAKES ALONG ITS BACK AND ANOTHER FOR ITS TAIL.

IN THE END HE BROUGHT HIM TO EURYSTHEUS WHO WAS, AS USUAL IN SUCH MOMENTS OF HEROISM, HIDDEN IN A PITHOS.

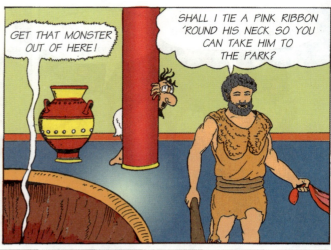

GET THAT MONSTER OUT OF HERE!

SHALL I TIE A PINK RIBBON 'ROUND HIS NECK SO YOU CAN TAKE HIM TO THE PARK?

BUT AS YOU KNOW, ALL GOOD THINGS COME TO AN END. WHEN HERACLES WAS MARRIED TO HIS SECOND WIFE DEIANEIRA...

YOU **CENTAUR**! YOU DARE TO LAY YOUR HANDS ON MY WIFE? I'LL KILL YOU FOR THAT!

IF YOU ARE EVER IN DANGER OF LOSING HIM, DEIANEIRA, SOAK HIS CLOTHES IN MY BLOOD.

DEIANEIRA, HERACLES SENT ME FOR SOME CLEAN CLOTHES BECAUSE HE WANTS TO MAKE A SACRIFICE TO ZEUS.

WAIT A MOMENT LICHAS, I'LL GIVE YOU A CLEAN ROBE.

THE BEAUTIFUL IOLE HAS STOLEN HIS MIND. WITH THIS MAGIC POTION OF THE CENTAUR, I'LL KEEP HIM CLOSE TO ME.

THE CLOTHES SHE SENT HIM STUCK TO HIS BODY AND BURNED HIM AND HE COULD NOT REMOVE THEM. HE PLEADED WITH HIS FRIENDS TO BURN HIM ON A PYRE. PHILOCTETES WAS A FOLLOWER OF EUTHANASIA AND WHEN HE LIT THE FIRE, HERACLES GAVE HIM HIS BOW AND ARROWS, THEN A CLOUD CAME DOWN AND RAISED THE DEMIGOD TO OLYMPUS...

...TO LIVE FROM THEN ON WITH THE GODS.

ANOTHER GREAT HERO WHO BECAME A HOUSEHOLD NAME WAS THESEUS. HE WAS BORN OF AETHRA, DAUGHTER OF THE KING OF TROEZEN AND HIS FATHER WAS AEGEUS, KING OF ATHENS.

FINE, AETHRA DIDN'T UNDERSTAND ANY-THING ABOUT THE FACTS OF LIFE, BUT WHAT ABOUT AEGEUS? WAS HE TOO DRUNK TO KNOW WHAT HE WAS DOING?

HE DIDN'T UNDERSTAND EITHER, EH?

NOT TO MENTION THAT WHEN HE LEFT HE PUT HIS SWORD AND HIS SHOES UNDER A BIG ROCK FOR HIS SON TO PICK UP WHEN HE GREW UP AND TO PUT ON SO HE WOULD RECOGNIZE HIM.

HOW COULD HE BE SO SURE THAT IT WOULD BE A BOY? THE TOURIST!

MANY YEARS LATER, THE BRAVE, STOUT-HEARTED YOUNG THESEUS, SON OF AETHRA, SET OUT FOR ATHENS TO FIND HIS FATHER, KING AEGEUS.

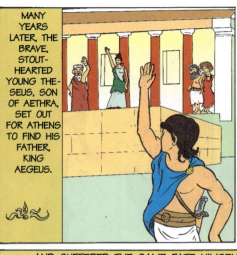

ALONG THE WAY HE KILLED A LOT OF BAD GUYS.

AH, PERIPHETES, EVER SINCE I WAS A KID I'VE WANTED HERACLES' CLUB, BUT YOURS WILL DO JUST FINE.

AAAAAA!

THE ROBBER, SINIS THE PINE-BENDER, TORE HIS VICTIMS IN HALF...

HA! HA! HA! NOT EVEN JACK THE RIP-PER DID THIS!

FREE CHOICE OF TREE

...AND SUFFERED THE SAME FATE HIMSELF.

NO TWO WAYS ABOUT IT, SINIS. YOU ALWAYS DID HAVE A SPLIT PERSONALITY.

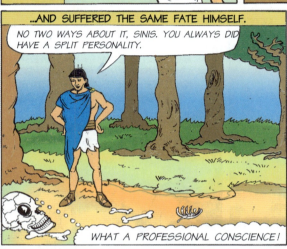

WHAT A PROFESSIONAL CONSCIENCE!

ANOTHER BAD GUY WAS SCIRON WHO SAT ON A NARROW CLIFF PATH ON THE SCIRONIAN ROCKS AND MADE PASSERS-BY WASH HIS FEET, AFTER WHICH...

PONGI PONGI

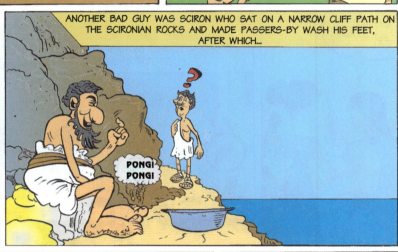

...WITH A KICK HE SENT THEM OVER THE CLIFF AND DOWN INTO THE SEA WHERE AN ENORMOUS TURTLE ATE THEM.

HA! HA! HA!

SLURP! SLURP!

DON'T YOU THINK IT'S YOUR TURN TO GIVE ME A PEDICURE?

THUS SCIRON RECEIVED THE SAME DEATH AS HIS VICTIMS.

HONEY, YOUR PARTNERSHIP HAS BEEN DIS-SOLVED, BUT YOUR SHELL WILL MAKE A WONDERFUL SHIELD.

ANOTHER CRIMINAL, PROCRUSTES, MADE STRANGERS LIE DOWN ON A BED. IF THEY WERE TALL, HE CUT THEIR FEET OFF AND IF THE WERE SHORT, HE STRETCHED THEM UNTIL THEY WERE EXACTLY THE RIGHT LENGTH.

PROCRUSTES' WORKSHOP OF ISOMETRIC ADJUSTMENTS

YOU DESERVE...PRAISE FOR...GIVING SO MANY TRAVELLERS A REST. BUT HAVE A LIE DOWN YOUR-SELF AND LET'S SEE HOW...COMFORTABLE YOUR BED IS.

AND SO HE TOO MET THE SAME DEATH AS HIS VICTIMS

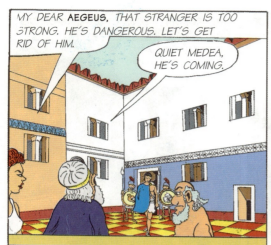

MY DEAR AEGEUS, THAT STRANGER IS TOO STRONG. HE'S DANGEROUS. LET'S GET RID OF HIM.

QUIET MEDEA, HE'S COMING.

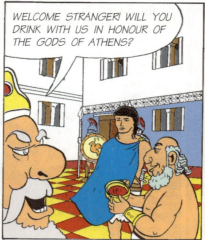

WELCOME STRANGER! WILL YOU DRINK WITH US IN HONOUR OF THE GODS OF ATHENS?

DON'T! BY ZEUS! YOU'RE MY SON.

FATHER, I'M SO HAPPY!

ONE DAY...

MY SON, THE TAX WE PAY TO CRETE IS VERY HEAVY. MINOS DEMANDS SEVEN YOUNG MEN AND SEVEN YOUNG WOMEN FROM OUR FINEST FAMILIES AS FOOD FOR THE MINOTAUR.

WHAT'S THE MINOTAUR?

WELL, MOST PEOPLE HAVE A HOUSE PET, MINOS HAS A MONSTER. A HALF-BULL HALF-MAN WHO LIVES IN THE LABYRINTH. A PALACE WHERE WHOEVER ENTERS CANNOT GET OUT FROM THE MANY CORRIDORS AND GALLERIES.

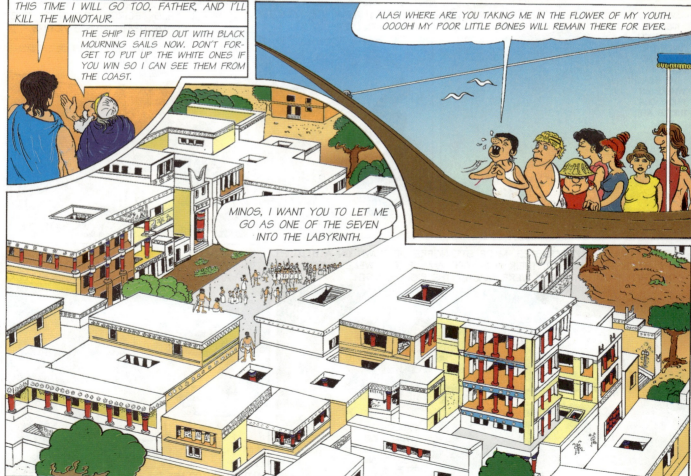

THIS TIME I WILL GO TOO, FATHER, AND I'LL KILL THE MINOTAUR.

THE SHIP IS FITTED OUT WITH BLACK MOURNING SAILS NOW. DON'T FORGET TO PUT UP THE WHITE ONES IF YOU WIN SO I CAN SEE THEM FROM THE COAST.

ALAS! WHERE ARE YOU TAKING ME IN THE FLOWER OF MY YOUTH. OOOOH! MY POOR LITTLE BONES WILL REMAIN THERE FOR EVER.

MINOS, I WANT YOU TO LET ME GO AS ONE OF THE SEVEN INTO THE LABYRINTH.

I HAVE NO INTENTION OF STOPPING YOU. BUT YOU CAN'T TAKE ANY WEAPONS.

BY APHRODITE! WHAT A HUNK!

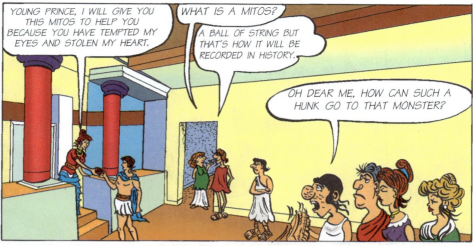

YOUNG PRINCE, I WILL GIVE YOU THIS MITOS TO HELP YOU BECAUSE YOU HAVE TEMPTED MY EYES AND STOLEN MY HEART.

WHAT IS A MITOS?

A BALL OF STRING BUT THAT'S HOW IT WILL BE RECORDED IN HISTORY.

OH DEAR ME, HOW CAN SUCH A HUNK GO TO THAT MONSTER?

SHHH! HE'LL HEAR YOU AND YOU KNOW FROM THE NECK DOWN HE'S A REAL MAN.

OOH! I ALWAYS FALL FOR THE MEAN ONES?

QUIET! HE'S COMING!

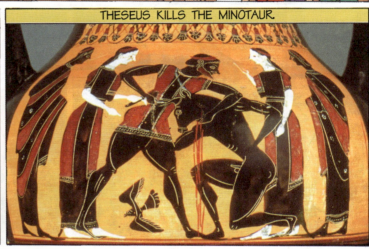

THESEUS KILLS THE MINOTAUR.

THEY ARE ALL HAPPY ON THE BOAT BACK TO ATHENS...

AREN'T I THE BRAVE ONE THOUGH! IF IT WASN'T FOR ME, THE MINOTAUR WOULD HAVE TORN YOU ALL TO SHREDS.

AEGEUS GAZES OUT TO SEA FROM SOUNION.

OH GODS! MY SON LOST.

IN ALL THE EXCITEMENT NO ONE REMEMBERED...

...TO CHANGE THE BLACK SAILS

THE PLACE WHERE AEGEUS JUMPED INTO THE SEA WAS SOUNION AND THE SEA WAS CALLED THE AEGEAN SEA FROM THEN ON. THESEUS SUCCEEDED HIS FATHER TO THE THRONE OF ATHENS AND GOVERNED IT JUSTLY FOR MANY YEARS.

I LIKE STORIES WITH MONSTERS. DO YOU KNOW ANOTHER ONE?

I'LL TELL YOU ABOUT A SPECIAL MONSTER, COMPLETELY DIFFERENT FROM THE OTHERS. MEDUSA, WHOM THE HERO PERSEUS KILLED.

POLYDECTES, RULER OF SERIFOS, WANTED TO GET CLOSER TO PERSEUS' MOTHER, THE BEAUTIFUL DANAE.

THAT CREEP! HOW CAN I GET RID OF HIM?

PERSEUS, I'M MAKING A COLLECTION AND SINCE YOU ARE FROM A NOBLE FAMILY, I WANT AN EXPENSIVE GIFT FROM YOU.

EXPENSIVE?!

HA! HA! WHAT ABOUT THE HEAD OF MEDUSA?

DONE!

BUT HOW?!

GO ON. GO ON.

MEDUSA WAS ONE OF THE THREE GORGONS, THE MOST FRIGHTENING. SHE HAD SNAKES FOR HAIR, THICK TUSKS FOR TEETH, SCALES ON HER NECK, AND WINGS. WHOEVER LOOKED AT HER WAS TURNED TO STONE. THE ONLY ONE WHO HAD EVER DATED HER WAS POSEIDON, THAT'S HOW UGLY SHE WAS.

NOW WHAT ARE THEY DOING?

THEY GAVE HIM WINGED SANDALS SO HE COULD MOVE SWIFTLY, THE HELMET OF HADES TO MAKE HIM INVISIBLE AND A SICKLE.

FORTUNATELY, HOWEVER, ATHENA AND HERMES OFFERED TO HELP HIM.

LOOK AT MEDUSA'S REFLECTION IN THE SHIELD AND YOU WON'T TURN TO STONE.

THE ENTRANCE TO THE CAVE WHERE MEDUSA LIVED WAS GUARDED BY THE GRAEA. THEY HAD ONLY ONE EYE BETWEEN THEM AND WHEN THEY CHANGED GUARD THE ONE WHO HAD IT GAVE IT TO THE NEXT. THUS PERSEUS...

CHANGE GUARD!

AAA!! THE EYE! THE EYE!

...RUSHED INTO THE CAVE WHERE MEDUSA WAS SLEEPING.

AS SOON AS HE CUT OFF HER HEAD, FROM THE GAPING NECK SPRANG THE HERO CHRYSAOR AND THE WINGED HORSE PEGASUS, FRUITS OF MEDUSA'S AFFAIR WITH POSEIDON.

BACK ON SERIFOS.

POLYDECTES! I'M BACK WITH YOUR GIFT.

HOW THE...???

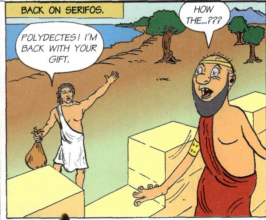

POLYDECTES AND ALL OF PERSEUS' ENEMIES WERE TURNED TO STONE AS SOON AS PERSEUS SHOWED THEM THE HEAD OF MEDUSA AND THAT'S HOW THE ISLAND OF SERIFOS CAME TO BE COVERED IN ROCKS.

AND HOW I CAME TO BE A STONECUTTER.

AS FOR THE DIVINE WINGED HORSE PEGASUS, POSEIDON GAVE IT TO ANOTHER OF HIS SONS, BELLEROPHON.

27

AND NOW I'LL TELL YOU THE STORY OF BELLEROPHON.

WHO WAS HE?

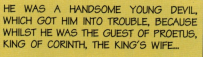

HE WAS A HANDSOME YOUNG DEVIL, WHICH GOT HIM INTO TROUBLE, BECAUSE WHILST HE WAS THE GUEST OF PROETUS, KING OF CORINTH, THE KING'S WIFE...

...FELL IN LOVE WITH HIM. BUT HE WAS STEADFAST!

HEY COME ON BIG BOY!

MADAM, PLEASE, I'M LIKE ONE OF THE FAMILY.

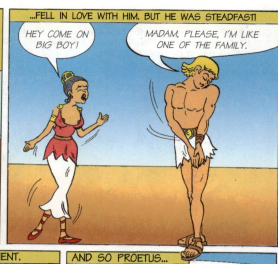

IN ORDER TO GET HER REVENGE, SHE ACCUSED HIM...OF SEXUAL HARASSMENT.

AND SO PROETUS...

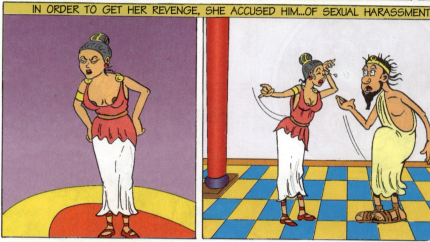

BELLEROPHON, I'VE BOOKED YOU AN EXCURSION WITH PEGASUS TOURS TO GO AND SEE MY FATHER-IN-LAW IN LYCIA.

THE KING'S FATHER-IN-LAW HAD INSTRUCTIONS TO GET RID OF HIM.

WELCOME YOUNG MAN, RIGHT ON TIME! I'VE ARRANGED A HUNT FOR YOU.

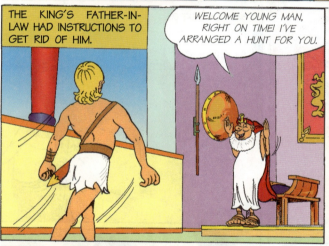

REALLY?! AND WHAT WILL I BE HUNTING?

HEH! HEH! HEH! THE CHIMERA!!

GULP!

THE CHIMERA, A TRULY DREADFUL AND FRIGHT-ENING MONSTER, LOOKED LIKE BOTH A GOAT AND A LION, HAD A SNAKE FOR A TAIL AND COULD SPIT FLAMES FOR A GREAT DISTANCE.

FORTUNATELY, BELLEROPHON HAD PEGASUS.

OH! OH! FLY HIGHER HORSIE, I CAN SEE US BOTH GETTING GRILLED.

BELLEROPHON SHOT HIS...

...ARROWS OFF FROM ON HIGH AND IN THIS WAY MANAGED TO KILL THE CHIMERA.

HE KILLED CRIMINALS...

...BATTLED THE AMAZONS...

...BECAME KING...

SOUVENIR OF THE CORONATION

...HAD A FAMILY...

FAMILY ALBUM

...BUT HIS VANITY DESTROYED HIM.

HIGHER HORSIE! FLY TO OLYMPUS SO THAT I CAN SEE THE DIVINE PALACES AND STAND BEFORE ZEUS.

AT ZEUS' COMMAND, THE DIVINE HORSE HURLED HIM DOWN FROM ON HIGH.

WE'D LIKE TO POINT OUT AT THIS POINT, THAT WHEN YOU HAVE A VEHICLE LIKE THAT, IT'S EASY TO ACCELERATE WITHOUT THINKING.

YOU SEE IT'S ALWAYS BEEN MAN'S DESIRE TO FLY LIKE A BIRD.

YES BUT HE MANAGED IT IN THE END.

WHAT AM SAYING??

SO YOU KNOW THAT ICARUS AND DEADALUS BECAME BIRDS?

WHAT'S THAT? WEREN'T WINGED HORSES ENOUGH, WE ALSO HAVE WINGED MEN?

WHEN ONE IS AN INVENTOR, YES.

THE ARCHITECT AND INVENTOR, DEADALUS, WAS IN EXILE ON CRETE DURING THE REIGN OF MINOS.

THE LABYRINTH AS WELL AS THE WHOLE PALACE WERE HIS WORK.

NICE PALACE YOUR HIGHNESS.

30

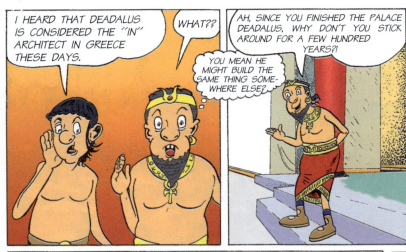

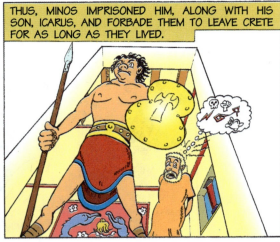

31

NOT SO HIGH!! THE SUN WILL MELT THE WAX!

NOT SO LOW! THE WAVES WILL GET THE WINGS WET!

BUT ICARUS DIDN'T LISTEN. AND SO THE ISLAND WHERE HE FELL IS CALLED ICARIA AND THE SEA, THE ICARIAN SEA.

BBZZZ

AND THUS THE POOR DAEDALUS FLEW OFF ALONE TO MAGNA GRAECIA*

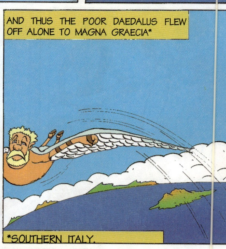

*SOUTHERN ITALY.

YOU RUINED IT FOR ME AGAIN. ALL THE GOOD MORTALS COME TO A NASTY END.

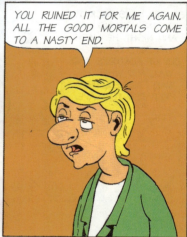

THAT'S THE WAY THE GODS WANT IT. BUT WAIT, I HAVEN'T TOLD YOU ABOUT OEDIPUS.

SO TELL ME. I REMEMBER THAT NAME FROM SOME-WHERE.

WELL...LAIUS, THE KING OF THEBES, GOT A PROPHECY FROM THE ORACLE THAT HE WOULD GET A SON WHO...

WILL KILL YOU AND MARRY HIS MOTHER.

WHAT??!

ORACLE "THE GOOD PROPHECY"

IN THEBES, A SHORT TIME LATER.

THE QUEEN HAD A SON!

LAIUS CALLED FOR ONE OF HIS SHEPHERDS.

TAKE THE BABY AND GO TO THE MOUNTAIN AND KILL HIM.

THE SHEPHERD TOOK PITY ON THE BABY AND LET IT LIVE, BUT HE GREW UP IN ANOTHER TOWN WITH DIFFER-ENT PARENTS.

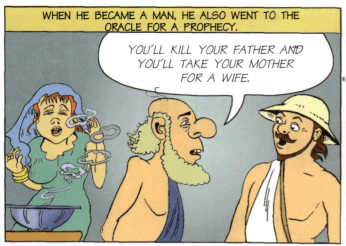

WHEN HE BECAME A MAN, HE ALSO WENT TO THE ORACLE FOR A PROPHECY.

YOU'LL KILL YOUR FATHER AND YOU'LL TAKE YOUR MOTHER FOR A WIFE.

SO THAT THIS WOULDN'T HAPPEN, HE LEFT HIS FOSTER PARENTS WHOM HE BELIEVED TO BE HIS REAL ONES.

HMM! NOW I REMEMBER WHAT IT REMINDED ME OF.

HEY! ALL THIS OPENED THE WAY FOR FREUD.

HE PERFORMED A GREAT MANY FEATS BECAUSE HE WAS A SPECIAL AND BRAVE YOUNG MAN.

BRAVOOOOO!

BUT ONE DAY, AT A CROSSROADS...

MAKE WAY FOR THE KING!

OEDIPUS IGNORED THEM AND STARTED TO PASS.

ILL-MANNERED RUF-FIAN! I'LL TEACH YOU.

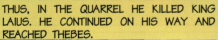

THUS, IN THE QUARREL HE KILLED KING LAIUS. HE CONTINUED ON HIS WAY AND REACHED THEBES.

THERE HE SOLVED THE RIDDLE OF THE SPHINX, A MAN-EATING MONSTER.

WHAT CREATURE WALKS SOMETIMES ON FOUR LEGS, SOMETIMES ON TWO LEGS AND SOMETIMES ON THREE?

A MAN.

STONE ME! HE GOT IT!!

AND SO THE SPHINX COMMITTED SUICIDE.

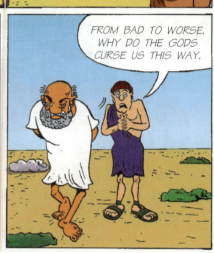

NOW I'LL TELL YOU ABOUT THE GREAT VOYAGE OF THE ARGONAUTS. WELL, IN IOLCOS, THE KING WAS PELIAS, USURPER OF THE THRONE. THE REAL KING, JASON, HIS BROTHER'S SON...

WAS RETURNING FROM PELION WHERE HE HAD BEEN STUDYING WITH THE CENTAUR CHIRON.

GOSH! PELIAS WILL BE SHAKING IN HIS BOOTS WHEN HE SEES HIM. THE PROPHECY SAYS THAT A ONE-SANDALED MAN WILL TAKE THE THRONE.

UNCLE, I AM NOW A MAN AND HAVE RETURNED TO ASSUME MY RIGHTFUL THRONE.

NOT UNTIL YOU BRING BACK TO IOLCOS THE GOLDEN FLEECE...

...OF THE RAM UPON WHICH OUR ANCESTOR, PHRIXUS, TRAVELLED.

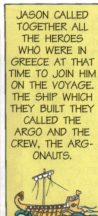

JASON CALLED TOGETHER ALL THE HEROES WHO WERE IN GREECE AT THAT TIME TO JOIN HIM ON THE VOYAGE. THE SHIP WHICH THEY BUILT THEY CALLED THE ARGO AND THE CREW, THE ARGONAUTS.

WELCOME HELMSMAN TIPHYS, WELCOME GREAT HERACLES AND ORPHEUS, THANK YOU ALL.

LOOK! THE SYMPLEGADES ROCKS, WHICH SMASH TOGETHER CONTINUOUSLY, THEY'LL CRUSH THE SHIP.

THE SEER PHINEAS SAID WE SHOULD RELEASE A DOVE TO SEE IF IT CAN MAKE IT THROUGH.

THE DOVE MADE IT! IT ONLY LOST A FEW TAIL FEATHERS.

OOH, MY LITTLE BIRDIE!

RIGHT! AS SOON AS THE ROCKS OPEN...ROW OR WE'LL BE LOST!

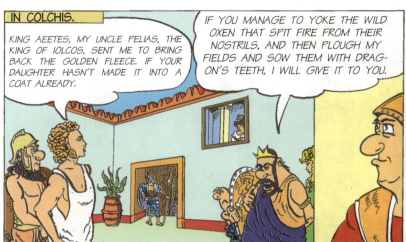

IN COLCHIS.

KING AEETES, MY UNCLE PELIAS, THE KING OF IOLCOS, SENT ME TO BRING BACK THE GOLDEN FLEECE. IF YOUR DAUGHTER HASN'T MADE IT INTO A COAT ALREADY.

IF YOU MANAGE TO YOKE THE WILD OXEN THAT SPIT FIRE FROM THEIR NOSTRILS, AND THEN PLOUGH MY FIELDS AND SOW THEM WITH DRAGON'S TEETH, I WILL GIVE IT TO YOU.

BECAUSE YOU'RE A GOOD LOOKING KID AND YOU HAVE A SHIP, I'M GOING TO HELP YOU IF YOU PROMISE TO TAKE ME WITH YOU ON YOUR NEXT CRUISE.

DEAL!

MEDEA GAVE JASON A MAGIC LOTION TO SPREAD ON HIS SKIN SO THAT THE FLAMES SHOOTING OUT OF THE OXEN'S NOSTRILS WOULDN'T BURN HIM. AS SOON AS HE PLANTED THE DRAGON'S TEETH, SOLDIERS IN FULL ARMOUR SPRANG FORTH.

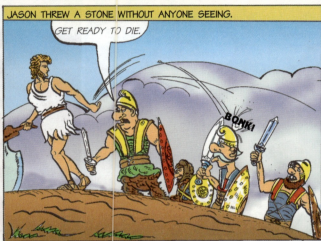

JASON THREW A STONE WITHOUT ANYONE SEEING.

GET READY TO DIE.

BONK!

DID YOU HIT ME? WELL TAKE THAT!

WHAT ARE YOU HIT-TING ME FOR? NOW YOU'LL SEE.

CLANG!

HEY! LET ME SPROUT FIRST!

THUS, ACCORDING TO MEDEA'S PLAN, THE SOLDIERS KILLED EACH OTHER.

THIS POWDER WILL PUT THE DRAGON TO SLEEP.

TO THE SHIP QUICK! THEY'RE AFTER US.

THE SIRENS LAY IN WAIT FOR SAILORS PASSING BY AND CAST A SPELL ON THEM TO MAKE THEM THEIR VICTIMS.

GET READY! WE'RE COMING UP ON THE SIRENS, IF THEY GET US IN THEIR CLAWS THEY'LL TEAR US APART.

GIRLS, THE FLEEET!

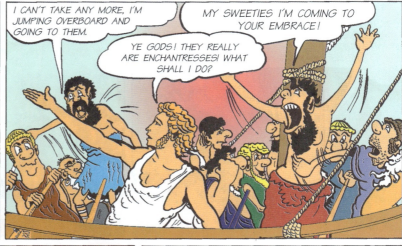

I CAN'T TAKE ANY MORE, I'M JUMPING OVERBOARD AND GOING TO THEM.

YE GODS! THEY REALLY ARE ENCHANTRESSES! WHAT SHALL I DO?

MY SWEETIES I'M COMING TO YOUR EMBRACE!

THEN ORPHEUS BEGAN TO SING.

THE YEARS HAVE PASSED ALONG WITH TIME.
BABIES HAVE GROWN TO YOUNG MEN IN THEIR PRIME.
PARENTS BY NOW ALL HAVE HAIR OF SNOW WHITE,
AND WIVES' SLEEPLESS HEADS LAY ON PILLOWS EACH NIGHT.
OH! SWEETEST HEARTH OF MY HOME-WARMING FIRE,
CHILDREN, SAD WIFE WHO IN FAITH NEVER TIRES,
I VOW TO THE GODS FROM AFAR TO RETURN
AND I AWAIT THE GREAT FEASTING UPON MY RETURN.

WE'RE WITH YOU ORPHEUS.

ORPHEUS, YOU'VE MADE THEM HOME-SICK.

BOO HOO HOO!

TO YOUR OARS FRIENDS. THE ARGO WILL TAKE US HOME!

IOLCOS

LONG LIVE JASON!

ORPHEUS PUT IT VERY NICELY, BUT I WAS DISTRACTED BY THOSE DARLINGS.

AND THUS THE ARGONAUTIC EXPEDITION RETURNED SUCCESSFULLY AND JASON ASSUMED THE THRONE OF IOLCOS.

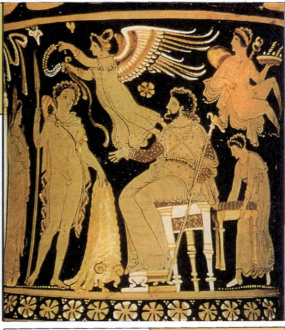

AND SPEAKING OF EXPEDITIONS, LET ME TELL YOU A LITTLE ABOUT THE TROJAN WAR WHICH THE GREAT POET HOMER MADE FAMOUS IN THAT MIGHTY EPIC 'THE ILIAD'.

37

HAVE YOU HEARD? PARIS, THAT LITTLE TOFF FROM TROY, WENT TO SPARTA TO STAY WITH KING MENELAUS AS A GUEST. HE WAS WINED, DINED AND ENTERTAINED AND MADE HIMSELF FEEL QUITE AT HOME. THEN, WHEN HE LEFT, HE KIDNAPPED THE KING'S WIFE.

OUTRAGEOUS! OUTRAGEOUS!

WAIT A MO. WASN'T MENELAUS MARRIED TO THE BEAUTIFUL HELEN? SHE'S A REAL PEACH.

OUTRAGEOUS! OUTRAGEOUS!

OUTRAGEOUS! OUTRAGEOUS! BUT HEY, THIS IS HELEN WE'RE TALKING ABOUT NOT JUST SOME AIR HEAD! ISN'T IT?

GOSH! I DON'T KNOW WHAT I WOULD HAVE DONE IN HIS PLACE...

BUT NOW WE'RE GOING TO WAR. AGAMEMNON, THE BROTHER OF THE OFFENDED PARTY, HAS STARTED ORGANIZING A CAMPAIGN. EVERYONE'S TAKING PART: THE ACHAEANS, THE AEOLIANS AND ALL THEIR KINGS AND TROOPS.

WE'LL TEACH THAT LITTLE SNEAK AND ANYONE WHO EVEN THINKS OF LAYING A HAND ON OUR WOMEN.

CLAP! CLAP!

THEOPHIBRONAS, WHAT WOULD YOU DO IF SOMEONE KIDNAPPED YOUR WIFE?

UUUH...I'D ADMIRE HIS COURAGE, MELIRITES WEIGHS A HUNDRED AND FIFTY KILOS!

BRAVE MEN, WE ARE SETTING OFF TO SHOW THE TROJANS WHAT'S WHAT...TO TEACH THEM THAT WE CAN TAKE THEIR WOMEN BUT THEY CANNOT TAKE OURS.

LONG LIVE AGAMEMNON! BRAVOOO!!!

BUT THE WIND WOULDN'T BLOW AND THE SEER CALCHAS SAID THAT THE GODDESS ARTEMIS WAS ANGRY WITH AGAMEMNON.

YOU HUNTED HER DEER!

ME! WHAT HAVE I DONE TO HER?

AND WHAT DOES THE GODDESS WANT NOW?

YOU MUST SACRIFICE YOUR DAUGHTER!

AGAMEMNON SHOUTED AND STAMPED AND FLEW INTO A RAGE BUT IN THE END HE GAVE IN, OTHERWISE THEY WOULD NEVER HAVE BEEN ABLE TO SET SAIL. HE LED IPHIGENIA TO THE ALTAR BUT THE GODDESS TOOK PITY ON HER AND PUT A DEER IN HER PLACE WHILST A CLOUD CAME DOWN AND TOOK IPHIGENIA AWAY.

FAVOURABLE WINDS BEGAN TO BLOW.

ACHILLES, THESE ARE THE WALLS OF TROY. TOMORROW WE WILL START THE SIEGE.

THAT WRETCHED BROTHER OF MINE! FANCY LEAVING YOUR WIFE ALONE WITH THAT BRONZED HUNK.

HE TROJANS ARE NOT GOING TO ENJOY THIS. LET US NOW HONOUR PROTESILAUS, OUR FIRST CASUALTY, WHO WAS KILLED BY HECTOR THE MOMENT WE LANDED.

MR. BUSINESSMAN, JUST THINK OF ALL THOSE BUSINESSES THAT WILL OPEN AS SOON AS TROY FALLS. TOLL BOOTHS. HOUSING ESTATES. HEH! HEH! HEH!

ACHILLES, THE BRAVEST OF ALL THE GREEKS, KNEW IT WAS HIS FATE TO DIE AT TROY.

GREAT ACHILLES, SON OF PELIAS, YOU DESERVE THIS LOVELY PRIZE. YOUR WIFE!

LUCKY GUY! BUT AGAMEMNON'S...WHAT A LOOKER.

HIC!

I AM CHRYSES, THE PRIEST OF APOLLO AND I HAVE COME TO ASK YOU TO GIVE ME BACK MY DAUGHTER, CHRYSEIS, WHOM YOU HAVE IN YOUR TENT.

LISTEN OLD MAN, I'M AGAMEMNON AND I'M THE VICTOR AND YOUR DAUGHTER IS MY PRIZE. I'M A HANDSOME GUY, I'VE BEEN AROUND SO WHAT MORE DO YOU WANT?

AGAMEMNON'S PRIZE WAS THE BEAUTIFUL CHRYSEIS.

AGAMEMNON THREW THE PRIEST OUT. THE GOD APOLLO GOT ANGRY AND SHOT AT THE ACHAEAN TROOPS FROM THE MOUNTAINS OF TROY.

AAEEEIIIII!

THUS AGAMEMNON WAS FORCED TO GIVE CHRYSEIS BACK. BUT HE MADE THE MISTAKE OF TAKING BRISEIS FROM ACHILLES.

YOU'RE WORTHLESS, NEVER THINK OF ANYONE BUT YOURSELF.

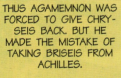

I AM THE LEADER OF YOU ALL AND I HAVE A RIGHT TO MY GIFT.

YOU HAVE TO TAKE MINE? TRY THINGS ON YOUR OWN FOR A WHILE AND YOU'LL FIND OUT WHAT I'M WORTH

...AND THE TROJANS SLAUGHTERED THE ACHAEANS.

CLANG!

ACHILLES, MY FRIEND, IS THIS GOING TO GO ON FOR LONG? THEY'RE WIPING US OUT. AT LEAST LET ME LEAD THE MYRMIDONES!

YOU THINK IT'S EASY FOR HIM? HE'S LOST HIS SPOILS.

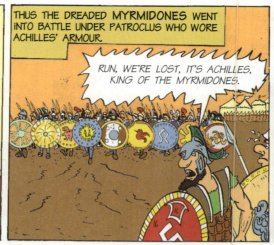

THUS THE DREADED MYRMIDONES WENT INTO BATTLE UNDER PATROCLUS WHO WORE ACHILLES' ARMOUR.

RUN, WE'RE LOST, IT'S ACHILLES, KING OF THE MYRMIDONES.

BUT HECTOR, LEADER OF THE TROJANS...

APOLLO TELLS ME IT ISN'T ACHILLES. I'M GOING TO ATTACK!

PATROCLUS WAS KILLED AND THERE WAS A FIGHT OVER THE BODY. MENELAUS FOUGHT TO GET IT AND THE ARMOUR.

BY THE NEXT BATTLE ACHILLES WAS BACK TO AVENGE HIS FRIEND. HE HURLED HIMSELF INTO THE FRAY.

HECTOR, DON'T GO BACK INTO BATTLE TODAY. THE OMENS ARE NOT GOOD.

SEER, I'M NOT A STAR-GAZER BUT A WARRIOR AND I DON'T LOOK TO SEE WHICH BIRD FLIES HIGHEST AND WHICH FALLS...

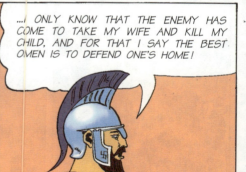

...I ONLY KNOW THAT THE ENEMY HAS COME TO TAKE MY WIFE AND KILL MY CHILD, AND FOR THAT I SAY THE BEST OMEN IS TO DEFEND ONE'S HOME!

DURING THE BATTLE ACHILLES SPIES HECTOR.

YOUR TIME HAS COME!

IS IT WORTH GOING UP AGAINST HIM?

ZEUS ON OLYMPUS.

HMM. THE BALANCE OF HECTOR'S FATE IS TILTING TOWARDS HADES.

ACHILLES KILLS HIM AND TAKES A HARSH REVENGE.

BUT THEN THE OLD KING, HECTOR'S FATHER, COMES TO REQUEST HIS BODY.

PRIAM I HAVE THE DEEPEST RESPECT FOR YOU. CONSIDER IT DONE.

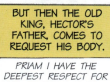

THE BATTLE CONTINUES.

IT'S AN ATTACK!

AAAAAA! THEY'RE BEHIND US.

HOW ABOUT A GAME OF BACKGAMMON DURING OUR BREAK ODYSSEUS?

COUNT ME IN AJAX.

THE ACHAEANS CRUSH THE TROJANS WHO ARE FORCED BEHIND THEIR WALLS. THEN THE GOD APOLLO APPEARS TO PARIS.

PARIS, ACHILLES' ONLY WEAK SPOT IS HIS HEEL. SHOOT HIM THERE!

PARIS HITS THE MARK.

A GREAT BATTLE BROKE OUT AROUND THE BODY OF ACHILLES.

ODYSSEUS, GLAUCUS IS TRYING TO STEAL THE BODY.

I'M RIGHT HERE AJAX.

FURTHER ON, PHILOCTETES KILLS PARIS.

ACHILLES WAS HONOURED AS A GOD.

WE'VE BEEN FIGHTING FOR NINE YEARS AND IT SEEMS LIKE IT WILL NEVER END. WE'VE LOST SO MANY MEN.

IT'S NOT FAIR BEING THRASHED AND HAVING YOUR WIFE CHEAT ON YOU.

I HAVE A PLAN.

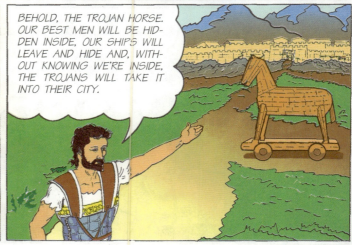

BEHOLD, THE TROJAN HORSE. OUR BEST MEN WILL BE HIDDEN INSIDE, OUR SHIPS WILL LEAVE AND HIDE AND, WITHOUT KNOWING WE'RE INSIDE, THE TROJANS WILL TAKE IT INTO THEIR CITY.

AS DAY BREAKS OVER TROY...

WHAT'S THAT?

THEY COULD SEE THEY WEREN'T GETTING ANYWHERE AND LEFT US A GIFT FOR THE GODS.

DON'T TRUST THEM! LEAVE IT OUTSIDE THE WALLS! IT WILL LEAD TO DISASTER.

LAY OFF, CASSANDRA. GET YOURSELF A MAN AND FORGET ABOUT PROPHECY.

THAT SAME NIGHT.

THEY'RE ASLEEP. LET'S GO!

OUCH! MY HIP'S SEIZED FROM ALL THAT SITTING.

CRRRACK!

CRRREEEAAAK!!

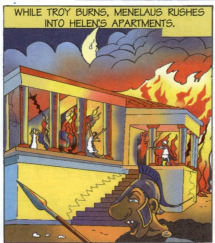

WHILE TROY BURNS, MENELAUS RUSHES INTO HELEN'S APARTMENTS.

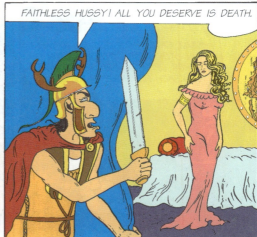

FAITHLESS HUSSY! ALL YOU DESERVE IS DEATH.

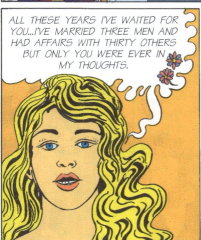

ALL THESE YEARS I'VE WAITED FOR YOU...I'VE MARRIED THREE MEN AND HAD AFFAIRS WITH THIRTY OTHERS BUT ONLY YOU WERE EVER IN MY THOUGHTS.

DID YOU REALLY MISS ME?

WHAT A JERK! TEN YEARS OF GETTING SLAUGHTERED FOR THAT?

SMACK! SMOOCH! SMOOCH!

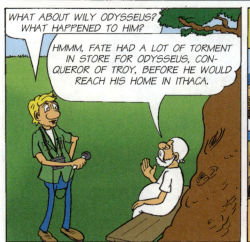

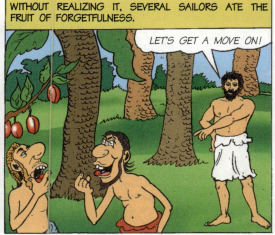

THEY HAD COME ASHORE IN THE LAND OF THE CYCLOPES; GIANTS WITH ONLY ONE EYE, WHO WERE STOCK-BREEDERS AND ATE HUMANS.

GREAT ZEUS ALMIGHTY!

CLOMP! CLOMP! CLOMP!

OOOOH! I DON'T BELIEVE MY EYES...UH...MY EYE!

HE'S SEALING THE ENTRANCE WITH A BOULDER. HOW WILL WE GET OUT NOW?

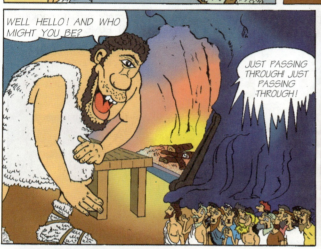

WELL HELLO! AND WHO MIGHT YOU BE?

JUST PASSING THROUGH! JUST PASSING THROUGH!

HO! HO! HO! WELL, AS A LITTLE WELCOME PRESENT, I'LL EAT A FEW OF YOU NOW!

SLUUUURP!!

MUNCH! SCRUNCH! MUNCH! SLURP!

DEAR GODS! HOW DISGUSTING!

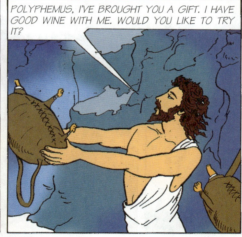

POLYPHEMUS, I'VE BROUGHT YOU A GIFT. I HAVE GOOD WINE WITH ME. WOULD YOU LIKE TO TRY IT?

GLUG! GLUG!

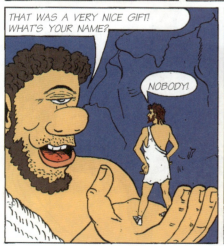

THAT WAS A VERY NICE GIFT! WHAT'S YOUR NAME?

NOBODY!

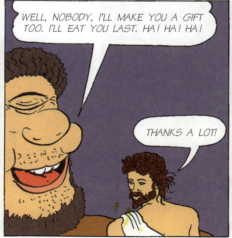

WELL, NOBODY, I'LL MAKE YOU A GIFT TOO. I'LL EAT YOU LAST. HA! HA! HA!

THANKS A LOT!

CAN YOU IMAGINE HOW MUCH MATERIAL IT WOULD TAKE TO MAKE HIM A PAIR OF UNDERPANTS?!

STOP MESSING ABOUT. WE'RE IN REAL TROUBLE. HE GOBBLED UP OUR MATES LIKE THEY WERE PEANUTS.

WE CAN'T EVEN GET AWAY NOW THAT HE'S DRUNK AND ASLEEP. THE DOOR'S CLOSED.

WHAT A SNORE. HE BELLOWS LIKE A BULL WHEN YOU STEP ON HIS BUNION.

I SAY LET'S KILL HIM!

IDIOT! WHO WOULD MOVE THE BOULDER THEN?

SMACK!

SO WHAT ARE WE GOING TO DO?

WE'LL BLIND HIM WITH THIS POLE.

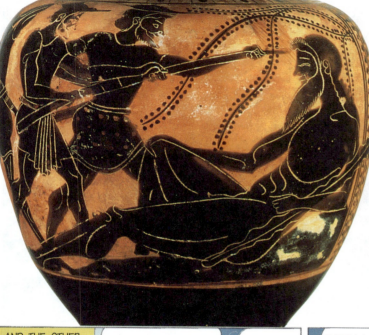

POSEIDON! AAARGH HEEELLLP!! THEY'VE BLINDED ME! COME QUICKLY!

AND THE OTHER CYCLOPES CAME.

WHO BLINDED YOU? WHO? WE'LL KILL HIM. TELL US HIS NAME.

NOBODY! NOBODY! BOO HOO HOO!

SHEESH! POLYPHEMUS HAS LOST HIS MARBLES.

WE GOT UP IN THE MIDDLE OF THE NIGHT FOR NOTHING.

LET'S GO BACK TO BED. IT'S MIDNIGHT AND ALL'S WELL.

IN THE MORNING.

HOLD ON TO THE SHEEP'S BELLIES AS THEY GO OUT OF THE CAVE BECAUSE THE MONSTER WILL BE SEARCHING FOR US.

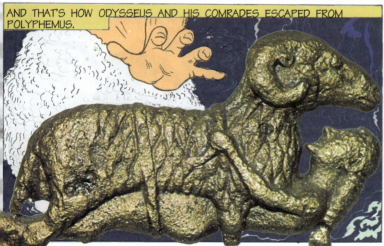

AND THAT'S HOW ODYSSEUS AND HIS COMRADES ESCAPED FROM POLYPHEMUS.

HEY POLYPHEMUS! IF ANYBODY ASKS WHO PUT OUT YOUR EYE, TELL THEM IT WAS ODYSSEUS, THE CONQUEROR OF TROY.

FATHER POSEIDON, I DEMAND REVENGE!

47

OH! TEN MEN CAME ASHORE
WINE IN POTS THEY BORE
THEY STOLE ME EYE FROM ME
THEN SCURRIED OFF TO SEA
GREAT MAST AND SAILS AWAKE
MY ANGER MAKES ME QUAKE
THEY DESTROYED MY DAYS SO SPRY
AND THE GIRLIES PASSING BY
WILL NO LONGER CATCH MY EYE.

SOBI SOBI

POOR DEVIL. AND HE WAS SINGLE TOO.

SPLOSH! SPLASH!

AFTER THE LAND OF THE CYCLOPES, THEY REACHED THE ISLAND OF AEOLUS, THE GOD OF THE WINDS. HE LIKED ODYSSEUS AND GAVE HIM AN OX-HIDE BAG.

ALL THE BAD WINDS ARE IN HERE. THE ONLY ONE FREE IS A GENTLE BREEZE WHICH WILL STEER YOU ALONG YOUR WAY.

AND WITH A FAIR WIND THEY CONTINUED OVER THE SEA.

ODYSSEUS IS ASLEEP AND THIS SKIN SMELLS LIKE RED WINE TO ME.

NO! DON'T TOUCH IT!

GO FOR IT MENANDRUS YOU OLD SOAK!

AND...WHAT A DISASTER! ALL THE WILD WINDS BURST OUT AND A STRONG TEMPEST ROSE UP WHICH NEARLY SANK THE SHIP.

PHHHEEEEEWWWW!! WE'VE BEEN COOPED UP FOR SO LONG.

THE WAVES TOOK THEM BACK TO THE ISLAND OF AEOLUS.

HONOURABLE AEOLUS, PLEASE PUT THEM BACK INSIDE ONCE MORE.

I'M SORRY BUT I DON'T WANT TO BECAUSE IT SEEMS THE OTHER GODS DON'T WANT TO HELP YOU.

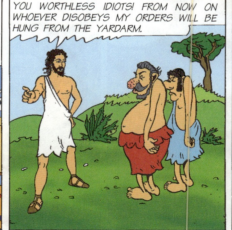

YOU WORTHLESS IDIOTS! FROM NOW ON WHOEVER DISOBEYS MY ORDERS WILL BE HUNG FROM THE YARDARM.

THE NEXT DAY.

LOOK! A LOVELY GREEN ISLAND.

HOW ODD! THE BOAT IS SAILING BY ITSELF AS IF DRAWN TOWARDS THE ISLAND BY MAGIC.

EURYLOCHUS, TAKE TEN MEN AND GO AND CHECK OUT THE ISLAND.

HELLO SAILORS! COME IN AND GET SOME REFRESHMENT.

ARE WE IN THE RED LIGHT DISTRICT?

I DUNNO, BUT I'D GLADLY DO A LITTLE ...SCIENTIFIC RESEARCH.

BUT AFTER THE MEAL, CIRCE, WHO WAS A WITCH, TOUCHED THEM WITH HER WAND AND TURNED THEM INTO PIGS.

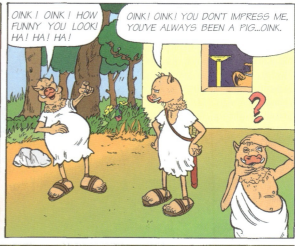

OINK! OINK! HOW FUNNY YOU LOOK! HA! HA! HA!

OINK! OINK! YOU DON'T IMPRESS ME, YOU'VE ALWAYS BEEN A PIG...OINK.

BEFORE SHE COULD TOUCH HIM, EURYLOCHUS ESCAPED AND WENT BACK TO THE SHIP.

OH DEAR! ODYSSEUS, THE WITCH CIRCE HAS TRANSFORMED OUR MATES INTO PIGS!

I SEE. THEN I'D BETTER GO AND INTRODUCE MYSELF.

BE CAREFUL ODYSSEUS.

SPLASH!

ON THE WAY THERE, HE MET THE GOD HERMES.

TAKE THIS MAGIC POTION AND SPRINKLE IT IN THE WINE CIRCE GIVES YOU. HER MAGIC CAN'T TOUCH YOU WITH THIS.

WELCOME ODYSSEUS!

ENOUGH OF THAT, WHERE ARE MY FRIENDS?

YOU'LL SEE THEM SOON. COME IN AND HAVE SOME WINE.

OINK! OINK!

GLUG! GLUG!

ZAP!

DIDN'T WORK EH? I'LL KILL YOU RIGHT NOW IF YOU DON'T PROMISE TO LIFT YOUR CURSE ON MY MATES.

DOOON'T! I'LL DO WHATEVER YOU WANT.

THE TOUGH GUY FOUND ME OUT!

AFTER HIS FRIENDS HAD BEEN TURNED BACK INTO MEN, THE FOLLOWING DAYS WENT REALLY WELL UNTIL THEY CONTINUED ON THEIR WAY AGAIN.

I'LL THINK VERY HARD BEFORE I EVER CALL SOMEONE A PIG AGAIN.

GET READY! WE'RE APPROACHING THE ISLAND OF THE SIRENS.

DON'T BE AFRAID. I'M GOING TO PLUG YOUR EARS WITH WAX SO YOU WON'T HEAR THEIR SEDUCTIVE SONG. LASH ME TO THE MAST. I WANT TO HEAR THEIR SONG, AND IF I ORDER YOU TO UNTIE ME, JUST MAKE THE ROPE TIGHTER.

49

JUST ONE SOLITARY MOMENT IS ENOUGH AND YOU WILL FIND,
IN THAT SINGLE SWEETEST MOMENT
THERE'S NO LOGIC IN YOUR MIND.
THERE'S A BEAUTIFUL EMBRACE THAT'S
FULL OF TENDERNESS AND MORE
THAT AWAITS YOU WHEN YOU LAND AND DISEMBARK UPON
THE SHORE.
AND IF AN HOUR LATER YOU SHOULD DIE AND CEASE TO BE,
YOU WILL FIND THERE IS ENOUGH IN WHAT YOU HEAR AND
WHAT YOU SEE.

WHAT A DIVINE MELODY! UNTIE ME YOU WORTHLESS FOOLS! YOU OLD SEA DOG, DON'T PLAY DUMB NOW!

THAT'S HOW THEY ESCAPED THE SIRENS AND THEY CONTINUED THEIR JOURNEY UNTIL...

WE'RE COMING IN ON SCYLLA AND CHARYBDIS.

SCYLLA WAS A MON-STER WITH THE HEAD AND BREASTS OF A BEAUTIFUL WOMAN BUT FROM THE WAIST DOWN SHE WAS SIX HUGE DOGS READY TO TEAR APART AND DESTROY ANYONE WHO WENT PAST. AS FOR THE MONSTROUS, CHARYBDIS, SHE SUCKED IN THE SEA AND SWALLOWED ENTIRE SHIPS WITH THEIR CREWS, THEN SHE WOULD SPIT THE SEA OUT IN ORDER TO...

...FOOL THE NEXT PASSING SHIP.

GLUG! GLUG! GLUG!

SO WHAT DO WE DO NOW?

SO THAT WE DON'T DROWN, WE'LL GO CLOSE TO SCYLLA ARMED TO THE TEETH AND HOPE THE GODS ARE WITH US...

SPLISH! SPLASH!

AS SOON AS CHARYBDIS HAD SPAT OUT THE WATER AND BEFORE SHE COULD SUCK IT IN AGAIN, ODYSSEUS' SHIP WENT THROUGH THE STRAITS ON SCYLLA'S SIDE. BUT THE MONSTER GRABBED FIVE OR SIX OF HIS MATES.

A FEW DAYS LATER.

LAND HO!

YIPPEE! WINE, WOMEN AND SONG!

CALM DOWN. YOU'LL NOT FIND ANY OF THAT ON THIS ISLAND. IT MUST BE THE ISLAND OF THRINACIE, WHERE THE CATTLE OF THE GOD HELIOS ARE KEPT.

CATTLE? OH BOY! I CAN SMELL THE BARBECUE ALREADY.

BETTER FORGET ABOUT THAT. THESE ARE SACRED CATTLE AND ARE DEDICATED TO THE GOD HELIOS. WOE BETIDE US IF WE HARM EVEN ONE HAIR ON THEIR HEADS!

THEY DISEMBARKED ON THE ISLAND TO TAKE ON WATER. THE SAILORS WERE STARVING AND WHILE ODYSSEUS WAS HAVING A NAP THEY SLAUGHTERED TWO OR THREE OF THE CATTLE AND ROASTED THEM ON SPITS.

IT'S ALWAYS BETTER TO DIE ON A FULL STOMACH.

MY DEAR, HUNGER IS A KIND OF TORTURE TOO.

SNIIIIF!

YE GODS! WHAT HAVE THOSE IDIOTS DONE?

PAFF!

SNACK?

HOW WILL WE ESCAPE THE RAGE AND THUNDERBOLTS OF ZEUS NOW?

...AS SOON AS THEY GOT OUT IN THE OPEN SEA A TERRIBLE STORM ROSE UP AND AT THE CRUCIAL MOMENT, ZEUS HURLED HIS THUNDERBOLT. THE SHIP BROKE UP, THE SAILORS DROWNED WHILST ODYSSEUS WAS SAVED BY CLINGING TO THE MAST.

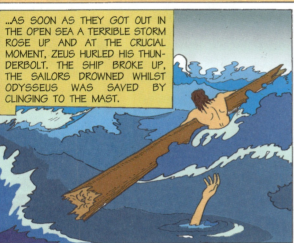

HE WAS AGAIN CLOSE TO CHARYBDIS. AT THE MOMENT SHE SUCKED IN WATER, HE MANAGED TO GRAB HOLD OF THE BRANCH OF A FIG TREE GROWING NEAR THE MONSTER'S CAVE.

HE BATTLED WITH THE WAVES FOR NINE DAYS UNTIL HE CAME TO THE ISLAND OF THE NYMPH CALYPSO.

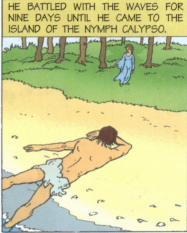

CALYPSO LIVED ON A VERY BEAUTIFUL ISLAND. SHE LOOKED AFTER ODYSSEUS AND HIS JOYFUL LIFE WAS LIKE A FAIRY TALE. SHE WANTED TO KEEP HIM AS HER HUSBAND AND GRANT HIM IMMORTALITY.

ODYSSEUS, YOO HOO!

OH OH! BACK TO WORK

BUT HE WAS PINING FOR HIS HOME IN ITHACA. ONE DAY HERMES, WHO WAS SENT BY ZEUS AND ATHENA, WENT TO CALYPSO...

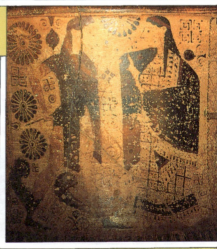

ZEUS ORDERS YOU TO LET HIM GO. HE HAS A HOME AND A FAMILY.

BUT WHAT ABOUT ME? HOW AM I SUPPOSED TO MAKE IT ALONE?

WHY MISS! YOU NEVER TOLD US YOU WANTED COMPANY!

CALYPSO BID HIM A RELUCTANT FAREWELL. HOWEVER...

...AS SOON AS POSEIDON SAW HIM SAIL OFF ON HIS RAFT, HE BLEW UP A STORM AND ODYSSEUS WAS AGAIN BATTLING THE WAVES. EXHAUSTED, HE REACHED THE ISLAND OF THE PHAEACIANS...

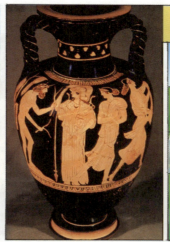

...AND NEXT TO THE RIVER HE MET NAUSICAA, THE KING'S DAUGHTER WHO HAD COME DOWN WITH HER SERVANTS TO WASH CLOTHES.

GIVE THE STRANGER SOME CLOTHES AND OIL SO HE CAN WASH IN THE RIVER.

MADAM WILL RUIN OUR REPUTATION!

AFTER HE HAD WASHED AND GOT DRESSED, ODYSSEUS PRESENTED HIMSELF TO HER, LOOKING SPLENDID.

WOW! WHAT A HUNK!

STRANGER, FOLLOW US TO MY FATHER'S PALACE. MAYBE WE CAN DO SOMETHING FOR YOU.

AT THE PALACE OF KING ALCINOUS.

YOUR FAME HAS REACHED EVEN HERE: WARRIOR, BRAVE, STRONG...

CHARMER AND ...A CASANOVA.

WELL I DO MY BEST.

OH OH! I SMELL AN ENGAGEMENT IN THE AIR.

YOU CAN STAY HERE FOR EVER, MARRY MY DAUGHTER AND THE THRONE WILL BE YOURS.

HOW CAN I EVER THANK YOU? THIS IS A GREAT HONOUR FOR ME, BUT FOR TWENTY YEARS I'VE BEEN LONGING TO SEE MY HOME IN ITHACA AGAIN. JUST TO SEE THE SMOKE RISING FROM THE CHIMNEY...

...FROM AFAR AND THEN TO DIE.

HA! HA! IF YOU DO EVER DIE.

THUS, ONE MORNING ALCINOUS AND THE PHAEACIANS BID FAREWELL TO ODYSSEUS. THEY SENT HIM TO ITHACA WITH THEIR OWN SHIP ALONG WITH...

...MANY EXPENSIVE GIFTS.

LET'S NOT WAKE HIM. WE'LL JUST LAY HIM GENTLY HERE ON THE SAND.

WAKE UP ODYSSEUS, YOU HAVE REACHED YOUR BELOVED ISLAND OF ITHACA, FROM WHICH YOU HAVE BEEN AWAY FOR TWENTY WHOLE YEARS.

OVERCOME WITH EMOTION, HE TOOK THE ROAD TO TOWN, STOPPING AT THE HUT OF HIS FAITHFUL SWINEHERD EUMAEUS.

MY KING! ALL THESE YEARS YOU'VE BEEN AWAY, NOBLEMEN FROM ALL OVER HAVE GATHERED AS...

...PROSPECTIVE SUITORS FOR YOUR WIFE. THEY EAT AND SQUANDER YOUR FORTUNE AND TRY TO GET YOUR SON OUT OF THE WAY.

AND...PENELOPE?

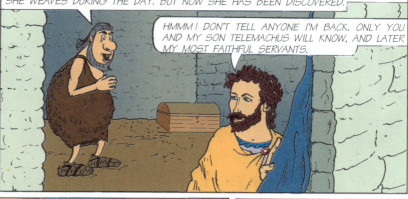

YOUR FAITHFUL SPOUSE LIVES WITH YOUR MEMORY. SHE TOLD THEM UNTIL YESTERDAY THAT SHE WOULD CHOOSE ONE OF THEM AS SOON AS SHE HAD WOVEN THE SHROUD OF THE OLD LAERTES, YOUR FATHER. SHE UNRAVELS EACH NIGHT WHAT SHE WEAVES DURING THE DAY. BUT NOW SHE HAS BEEN DISCOVERED.

HMMM! DON'T TELL ANYONE I'M BACK. ONLY YOU AND MY SON TELEMACHUS WILL KNOW, AND LATER MY MOST FAITHFUL SERVANTS.

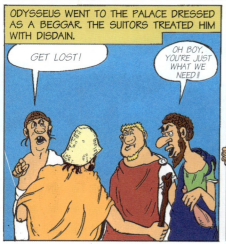

ODYSSEUS WENT TO THE PALACE DRESSED AS A BEGGAR. THE SUITORS TREATED HIM WITH DISDAIN.

GET LOST!

OH BOY, YOU'RE JUST WHAT WE NEED!!

THE NEXT DAY.

PENELOPE!

HI BEAUTIFUL!

HERE I AM MY LITTLE TURTLE DOVE!

MAKE UP YOUR MIND! I'M THE ONE FOR YOU.

GENTLEMEN, TODAY I HAVE FOUND A SOLUTION. I HAVE ORGANIZED A CONTEST.

WHOEVER MANAGES, WITH THE BOW OF MY HUSBAND, ODYSSEUS, TO SHOOT AN ARROW THROUGH THE HOLES OF NINE AXES SET UP IN A ROW, WILL BECOME MY HUSBAND!

THINGS DON'T LOOK GOOD FOR THE GROOMS!

THE FIRST TRIES. NO LUCK!

LEODES IS OUT!

EURYMACHUS IS OUT!

ANTINOUS, ANTINOUS...ANT...IS OUT!

SOME GUY THAT ODYSSEUS.

THEN THE BEGGAR ASKED TO HAVE A GO.

SOME GROOM! HA!-HA!

HA! HA! HA!

ODYSSEUS PULLED BACK THE BOW WITH EASE AND PUT HIS ARROW THROUGH THE NINE AXES. THEN...

...HE CAST OFF HIS RAGS.

ANTINOUS, THIS ARROW'S GOT YOUR NAME ON IT!

ODYSSEUS!!!

A BATTLE FOLLOWED. ODYSSEUS, WITH TELEMACHUS AND HIS FAITHFUL FRIENDS AND SERVANTS KILLED THE SUITORS.

AFTERWARDS HE TOLD THE FACTS TO A DOUBTFUL PENELOPE.

WIFE, I'M BACK.

IS IT REALLY YOU?

AND IF IT IS, DO YOU STILL SNORE?

WHAT'S THE WORLD COMING TO! A MAN CAN'T EVEN STEP OUT OF HIS HOUSE FOR TWENTY YEARS!

I'VE BEEN THROUGH SO MUCH AND I CAN'T FIGHT ANYMORE...I'M TIRED.

THEN I'LL MAKE YOUR BED SO YOU CAN GET SOME REST. IT'S OUTSIDE THE HALL.

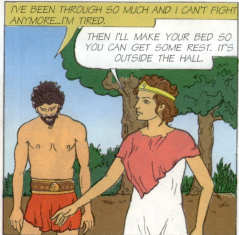

WHO COULD MOVE MY BED THAT I CARVED INTO THE THICK TRUNK OF A TREE WHOSE ROOTS GO DEEP INTO THE FOUNDATIONS OF THE PALACE?

ODYSSEUS! YOU REALLY ARE BACK!

THE NEXT DAY, ODYSSEUS WENT TO SEE HIS OLD FATHER WHO HAD GIVEN UP HOPE. AND THAT'S IT.

THANK YOU FOR WHAT YOU TOLD ME. I FOUND IT VERY INTERESTING.

54

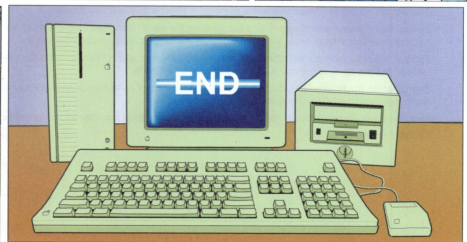

Glossary

Actaeon: *son of Aristaeus, the son of Cyrene, who was taught the art of hunting by the Centaur Chiron.*

Aegeus: *he saw the sword and sandals and recognized his son.*

Amazons: *a race of warrior women.*

Atlas: *son of the Titan, Iapetus.*

Augean Stables: *Augeas, son of Helios, was king of Elis in the Peloponnese. He had many herds but neglected to clean the manure from the stables and was in danger of infecting the whole country.*

Cattle of Geryon: *the monstrous Geryon had countless herds of cattle which were guarded by the shepherd Eurytion and the two-headed dog Orthrus, brother of Cerberus, the lion of Nemea and the Lernaean Hydra. Heracles killed Orthrus and stole the precious cattle.*

Centaurs: *monsters, half man (from the waist up) and half horse. Nessus was a bad Centaur.*

Ceryneian Hind: *this hind from Arcadia had golden horns and was dedicated to Artemis.*

Chiron: *Chiron was a good and wise Centaur. He had a school where the greatest heroes studied.*

Chrysippus: *son of Pelops.*

Cretan Bull: *this bull was able to spit flames from its nostrils as a result of Poseidon's revenge on Minos.*

Curetes: *demons worshipped with orgiastic ceremonies in Crete. Rhea entrusted the safe keeping of the infant Zeus to them.*

Erymanthian Boar: *a terrible boar living on Erymanthus, a mountain southwest of Arcadia.*

Ganymede: *son of Tros (who gave his name to the Trojans) and of Callirhoe, daughter of Scamander.*

Giants: *the Giants were huge cratures with snakes for hair and bodies ending in a dragon's tail.*

Girdle of Hippolyta: *as a symbol of her power, Hippolyta, queen of the amazons, wore a girdle of gold and precious stones.*

Golden Apples of the Hesperides: *at the foot of Mount Atlas was the garden of the Hesperides with the trees that bore golden apples. Because the daughters of Atlas were stealing these apples, Hera placed the trees under the protection of an immortal dragon with a hundred heads, and the Hesperides.*

Horses of Diomedes: *Diomedes, king of Thrace, had in his possession carnivorous horses which fed themselves on the flesh of passers by.*

Iolaus: *a nephew of Heracles'.*

Land of the Cicones: *located on the coast of Thrace. The Cicones were allies of the Trojans.*

Land of the Cyclopes: *believed to have been Sicily.*

Land of the Lotophagi (Lotus Eaters): *located on the coast of Africa, its inhabitants welcomed Odysseus and his companions hospitably.*

Lernaean Hydra: *The hydra of Lerna was a monster with a hundred heads which sprang forth from a twisted body.*

Lichas: *a companion of Heracles'.*

Myrmidons: *once ants, they were transformed into human beings to create the kingdom of Phthia ruled by king Peleus.*

Nemean Lion: *a supernatural being, a monster which struck fear and terror into the people of Nemea.*

Orpheus: *the son of Oeger and possibly of the muse Calliope. Charismatic musician, poet and singer.*

Othrys: *a mountain which separates the geographical regions of eastern Sterea Ellada and Thessaly.*

Pandora: *in the beginning she was an iron statue, but she was so beautiful that Zeus decided to give her life.*

Pegasus: *a winged horse, the child of Medusa and Poseidon. Poseidon offered it as a gift to Bellerophon who was also his son.*

Pherae: *on his trip to Thrace, Heracles stopped in Pherae and rescued Alcestis from Thanatos.*

Sirens: *sea demons with the body of a female from the waist up the rest, that of a bird. With their magical songs, they seduced passing travellers whose ships were smashed on the jagged rocks, thus providing the sailors as food for the Sirens.*

Sphinx: *a female monster with the head of a woman, the feet and tail of a lion and the wings of a bird of prey. She tortured the town of Thebes by eating those who could not solve her riddle.*

Stymphalian Birds: *predatory birds that lived on the banks of Lake Stymphalus in Arcadia. They had feathers made of steel so sharp that they used them like arrows on their enemies.*

Symplegades Rocks: *moving rocks which drew apart and then together again, smashing between them any passing ships.*

Titans: *brothers of Cronus.*